How She Hopes

DISCOVERING LIGHT IN THE DARK SEASONS OF YOUR LIFE

COURTNEY DUMLAO

The
Adonais
Properties

FOREWORD
BY JOHN DEMELLO

In this day and age so many people face the stress and demands of our fast paced society. We must struggle with seasons of discouragement and confusion. I believe that this book contains keys on how to identify and navigate these seasons that we all encounter. Courtney has approached this common condition with a transparency seldom found in other books. I have always been one to appreciate the value of truth conveyed in an applicable way. Simple and real is how I would characterize this book. Courtney is a spiritual daughter of our ministry and we are so proud to see her grow into her own potential and now help others along in their life's journey. I strongly encourage everyone who reads this book to be ready to grow into your own potential as well.

PRAISE FOR

How She Hopes

"Powerful words that bring healing and transformation! Courtney is a compelling teacher and advocate for women. She sheds light on dark shadows of the heart that long for light."

Dr. Jasmine Therese Esguerra, DC
Founder of Pure Wellness LLC,
The Well Made Foundation and Living Love Inc.

"A bold, inspiring read, opening the minds and hearts of readers both young and old to embrace their current season with courage and strength."

Patrick Snow
Publishing Coach and International Best-Selling
Author of Creating Your Own Destiny

"I absolutely love it! Such a powerful message that anyone can relate to. Courtney's stories are gripping and comforting at the same time. Anyone who reads this book will find the beauty in their particular season"

Brandi Saragosa

"This is the book I wish I had when I first came to know the Lord and through every subsequent storm I faced. Courtney manages to firmly yet lovingly hold your hand as you face some of your toughest moments. Her stories, insights and words are not only relatable, but find a way deep into your heart as she plants seeds of hope and restoration. Be ready to laugh, cry and most importantly learn to lean on the Lord and His promises"

Hannah Davenport

"I love how personal Courtney gets with her testimony, it's simple but powerful. Loved the prayers at the end of each chapter!"

Renata Awong

"Courtney opens up her heart to you, the reader, as she gently guides you to search your heart and find the path that leads you to experience your own healing, acceptance, hope, trust, forgiveness, faith, and eternal love."

Christy Fernandez, CSR, RPR

"Courtney has the ability to empower and encourage women. Her raw honesty reminds me that I have already won every battle through Christ! I love sitting in her kitchen as we discuss careers, spirituality and womanhood. Never afraid of a challenge, Courtney continues to lift others up as she charges forward in life."

Jen Kjellesvik
Owner/Outdoor Guide of Adventure Fitness LLC

Courtney is an amazing writer who speaks to your heart. With her strong faith in God, she allows him to show her the way while remaining humble, compassionate and caring. Her words are always inspiring, honest and on point.

Judina Haas

How She Hopes
Discovering Light in the Dark Seasons of Your Life

The Adonai's Properties ~ Hawaii

Copyright © 2021 by Courtney Dumlao

ISBN 978-0-578-72945-9

ISBN 978-0-578-84355-1

Published by The Adonai's Properties LLC
Book design by Jocelyn Designs, LLC
Editor: Sarah Thuerk

HowSheHopes.com

This book is dedicated to my husband, Kevin.

You are still my computer love.

For supporting our family and
being by my side always.

Kevin, Keola, Carson and Khloe- your humor,
grace, forgiveness and patience is God given.
I appreciate and love you more and more each day.

I love you always and forever.

I also dedicate this book to my children,
Keola, Carson, and Khloe. May you always
find hope in every season of your lives.

And I dedicate this book to you, the reader.
It is my heart's desire that this book brings
you the hope and confidence for tomorrow
that you are searching for today.

ACKNOWLEDGEMENTS

Shannie Akau
Rodney Akau
Renata Awong
Hannah Davenport
Kelli Delperdang
Randy Delperdang
John DeMello
Marian DeMello
Mary Delperdang
Carson Dumlao
Keola Dumlao
Kevin Dumlao
Khloe Dumlao
Jasmine Esguerra
Tricia Evans
Ellen Federoff
Christy Fernandez
Judina Haas
Christina Honokaupu
Jocelyn Johnson
Jen Kjellesvik
Vangie Ramos
Tiana Raymondo
Brandi Saragosa
AJ Sartalamacchia
Patrick Snow
Sarah Thuerk
The Ohana at In His House of Restoration
No Ka Oi Toastmaster Club Members

CONTENTS

INTRODUCTION

You would never know by the sparkle in her eye, or the playful smile she wears, that despair threatened to overtake her life. Many look upon her and wonder how she hopes for a brighter tomorrow when today looks so dark. It is her foundation of faith that keeps this courageous woman bold in her daily walk.

What you do not see is the seasonal impact of trial and error on this woman. Each season she has come through changed her sparkle. She is not perfect. She has, at times, lost her focus on the source of her hope. But she overcame that season of despair and so can you.

In this book are tools to help you find hope and learn how to persevere through the various seasons of life. Each chapter has a tool to help you navigate the darkness to find the light. For who hopes for what they see? It is through our faith, in hoping for what we do not see in the darkness that allows the light to break through.

You are not alone in this process of breakthrough. I, too, have stood in the light and soaked in the warmth and joy of the moment, only to have the day turn into a season of bitter darkness. Hope gives us the power to harness the dark; the faith you use to grow hope conquers that darkness.

The purpose of the pain is may be unknown for now. It may feel like the darkness is overtaking your mind and heart, but you are stronger than you know. You are brave enough to let go of the pain and take the necessary step toward hope. This oftentimes is the hardest part of the healing process. That first step requires you to let go of the security blanket of pain, and to surrender to the vast freedom of hope. It can be a hard step to take, but not impossible. You can do this. Are you ready? Are you ready to be set free from fear and the burden of pain? God did not allow your story to end today for a reason. He does not want you to carry the burden of pain. He wants you to glow with the light of love and hope. After all, it is contagious … it is time. Let your light shine, sister!

Let's spark a fire of hope with prayer:

Dear God,

Here I am. I am seeking peace and comfort in exchange for the pain and heartache of seasons past. I thank you for the lessons learned during those seasons. I thank you for the opportunity to start fresh today. I thank you for the healing that has already begun to take place in my heart, mind, soul and body as I surrender to your will for each upcoming season of my life. I thank you for those you have placed in my path to guide, protect, help, and love me. Help me to be aware of your holy presence as I am made new and my hope in you is restored. I thank you, Lord, for all that you are doing in my life to strengthen, sustain, and fulfill me. I pray that I am a blessing to others as I become a conduit of your love as you shine through me in all my future seasons.

In Jesus' name I pray...

Amen

CHAPTER 1

IDENTIFYING YOUR SEASON

*"There is a time for everything, and a season
for every activity under the heavens."*

Ecclesiastes 3:1

EMBRACING THE SUCK

My sanity was questionable as I entered empty nest stage one. There was no other option but to embrace the suck as I watched my son load his bags into the back of my silver minivan. As we drove, sniffling in sobering silence, the dawn broke over the mountain, a glorious display of oranges, pinks and blue filling the sky. The summer morning promised a gorgeous day. Yet my family was experiencing a loss and change that we were not quite ready for. You see, my oldest had just graduated high school two weeks prior. He was on his way to basic training for the U.S. Army, five thousand miles away from home. We knew once he landed we probably would not hear from him for a few weeks, and only through good old-fashioned, pen-pal letters. A part of my identity was boarding that plane, changing not only the trajectory of his future, but mine too.

My son, leaving for basic training, was the same age I was when I found out I was having him. The sobering reality that my identity as a mother and as a woman was so tied up in my son and other children caused me to panic. Letting him go felt like letting go of myself, and it was scary. It wasn't just me—my entire family was entering a new season of life and I had no idea how to cope with the loss of his presence in our day-to-day lives.

I knew that this is what God had intended for him. I was so excited for his own experience that I had not thought about what it would mean for me and the rest of my family until the day we had to drop him off at the airport. He was officially no longer just my son, but a member of the U.S. Army, and now under their jurisdiction and not my own.

After our tearful goodbyes, we made our way home and each of us went to our rooms to cry out our emotions. It was then, I realized, I have two options: I can be dragged down by my own despair or I can rise up and do something about it. I'd like to say I rose up right away, but I didn't. I'm stubborn and it took a while for me to process my emotions. I had no choice but to embrace the suck for the moment, and I did. I wallowed in my sorrow for a good few days and then I awoke to this quote by John Rohn:

"You must take personal responsibility. You cannot change the circumstances, the seasons, or the wind; but you can change yourself. That is something you are in charge of." This season I was experiencing I could not change, but I could change my outlook. Instead of looking inward at myself, I began to look up, to God, and I started to see him in a new light.

STARTING A NEW SEASON

Dark gray clouds hover and brisk winds roll over the grass. The air is damp, yet no rain is falling from the spring sky. Winter is refusing to let go of change, but spring has arrived, ready to take over. The two seasons clash, each one determined to have its way, one withholding change, and one determined to cause change. With every seasonal shift a storm will brew. The clashing of hot and cold air in the upper atmosphere creates a sensational changeover with each transition.

The blending of the old and new creates an uncomfortable season on the earth and in the air. It makes perfect sense then, that we humans become uncomfortable as we experience change. Out with the old and in with the new is intimidating for some and exhilarating for others. With a change of seasons comes a change with the reality of time. The daily schedule may be adjusted. Some shifting may be out of your control, such as the changing of the clocks; you do it because you must. However, some changes you are in charge of. You have a choice to cultivate your new season and to adjust to the atmosphere you are now in. There is no one more capable of cultivating this new season than you. You can choose to nurture this season into one of prosperity or let it wither to one of decrease; it all depends on how you prepare yourself mentally and physically. The first step for preparation is to identify your season and determine what it means to be the cultivator of it.

Now, I am sure you are wondering, how do you prepare for the unexpected shifts of a season? The unexpected loss of a loved one? The end of a marriage? The child gone too soon? The loss of a job? Addictions? The relationship that ended? How do you prepare for betrayal and heartache? You don't. That's right, you don't. You can't. It is too great a burden to prepare for, and no matter how prepared you think you are for that season of loss or change, it still hits like a tornado on a beautiful early spring day and destroys your routine. However, you can identify that the season of destruction, loss, and pain is temporary. That you are not alone. That you truly can overcome all things through Christ who strengthen you (Philippians 4:13). You lean into his strength and stop trying to rely on your own strength for the moment. You declare that what God has allowed, what the devil meant for evil, God intends for good. It may not look like it at the moment. It will come when you surrender to the season, when you accept that, yes, this major shift has occurred in your life. Now, how do you move forward? How do you use this pain to help someone else in the future?

SPRING IS STARTING

As a mama hen steers her chicks through the garden, the sun peeks over the mountain top a few minutes earlier today than last week. Spring is here. The beginning of new life speaks of hope and goodness to come. The heaviness of winter has passed. The days are getting longer and the air is warmer. It is a time to savor the steamy coffee outside with the rays of sunshine rather than from inside looking out the window. The time to be a spectator in life is over. It is time to go outside and be a part of it.

This is a time of great celebration in many cultures. The late Robin Williams once said, *"Spring is nature's way of saying, 'Let's party!'"* and I could not agree more. Think about it: way before electricity and technology, if you made it through the winter it was a testimony to your strength and vitality. Then, as the spring progresses, the rains come. As it nourishes the ground, the plants absorb the water. Our hearts are just like the ground, in need of refreshing. This is done through the word of God (John 7:37-39) and it is needed in the seasons to come. You may feel your soul needs life-giving water to thaw out the ice in your heart from the winters past. I want to encourage you. Just as the temperatures rise when spring transitions into summer, so must you adjust your internal spiritual thermostat to continue to thrive in your new season: it is time for spring to surrender to the blistering heat of summer.

SLIDING INTO SUMMER

Summer is arguably the most loved season of the year by many. It is full of vacations, fun, and soaking up vitamin D. Bright colors at the pool and maybe a sweet iced drink in the evening on the porch cheer up almost everyone. Summer weekends at our home mean sand-covered floor mats and kids laughing or bickering, in the backseat. Sun-kissed skin slathered in sunscreen; a trunk filled with coolers, beach chairs and large tote bags of towels, lotion, snacks and speaker. As I sit and watch my children play in the water and build sand towers, life feels gloriously simple and unhindered ... for a minute. Cue DJ skipping the vinyl. Last summer, when I experienced empty nest stage one, I did just this: sat at the beach, watched the kids, played the music ... but it was not the picture-perfect days I just listed. Oh no, this time was different. We did all the same activities, I even had more time with them, but the colors and sounds seemed dull. Life just was not the same and I truly struggled with my favorite family activities. I felt fragile, lost, and alone, not for the first time in life, but it was different this time.

That same summer, like many communities around the world, we experienced extreme wildfires burning a little too close to home. It was amazing to watch the infernos from a safe distance of many miles away. In wonder we speculated at what the fires would mean for the brush and wildlife that were in the vicinity. The impurities of past harvests were being burned up, clearing the way for new life in the next season. This refining of the ground is actually good for vegetation and farming. In fact, it plays a critical role in influencing vegetation and the life cycles of trees and plant communities. If the intense heat of the fire is good for the ground, I wondered, is this intense pressure of change, in this season, good for my soul? And the answer is yes. Yes, my friend, the pressure of change and the intensity from the heat in our souls, hearts, and minds is good for us. It allows us to grow and mature and more importantly, heal.

FINDING FALL

Have you been to a valley in the fall? The harvest of colors from the spring and summer rains are incredible. The rusts, reds, and yellows are breathtaking.

> *"Autumn carries more gold in its pocket than all the other seasons,"*
>
> Jim Bishop

The intense, stifling heat of summer ebbs away and the refreshing wind of the fall descends. Days become shorter, the nights longer. The late Billy Graham once said, "Mountains are for views and inspiration, but fruit is grown in the valleys." The season of harvest is upon the nation. The abundance from crops planted in the spring is now in full array, ready for winter storage.

What are you harvesting this fall season? After all, fall is known as a season of gratitude and appreciation. For farmers who lived off the land, their gratitude came from the successful harvest of their plantings months prior, which meant their survival in the cold months to come. Self-examination of our actions, hearts, and attitudes will reveal much about the seeds we have planted in seasons past. Recognizing our own internal dialogue that does not serve us is one of the first steps in finding hope for tomorrow's season. Winter is coming, and you need to be prepared for it or it will blindside you and leave you without the resources to withstand the bitter cold.

WONDERING IN WINTER

Scrolling social media, I see my loved ones across the nation bundle themselves with gloves and snow boots, carrying ice scrapers to their cars, and pictures of thermostats that read 9 degrees. And I think to myself, "God bless them, I could not handle that kind of winter." I would not be prepared. Shuffling to my car for my morning commute, I usher my daughter to the car door. Goosebumps dance across my arms as I fold into my seat and start the car. We close our doors, I push the button, start the engine, and read the thermostat on my car … 59 degrees … holy mother, winter is here! Yes! Do you know what that means? Tomorrow, I can wear boots!

Shorter days and longer nights make for this crisp, cool, Maui morning, and I love it. But the reality of it is, this is a season of preparation. It is cold outside in the mornings now; I need to make sure my daughter has her jacket and I need my hot coffee. Christmas is soon, so I need to shop and prepare for that too. As a person who plans almost every occasion and day to the brink of military time, winter reflects what we should be doing all year long, preparing for the next season. During this winter season, life seems to not be blooming. The ground is hard, green grass has turned brown for many. Snow covers what was bright green during the summer. With each December 31, many wonder what the New Year will bring them. Some doubt anything good or new, while others are perpetually optimistic and hope for exciting new changes. This season is less about the big moves of planting and harvesting and more about the small steps of planning to lay the foundation for the next harvest.

TRANSITIONING

Finding hope for the new season may feel exhausting or hopeless at this point. I understand, truly. But you cannot stay there. You must surrender that feeling that you won't find hope. Hope is there, but you are hanging on so tightly to the despair you are unable to see the light trying to peek through. When you abandon the despair, the light will be visible to you. I promise.

"No winter lasts forever; no spring skips its turn."

Hal Borland

Surrender is the catalyst to the evolving season of growth and change. Fighting the change, refusing to surrender to it, no matter the circumstances, will only encourage fear, doubts, anger, resentment, and pain.

Your time on earth is not meant to be permanent. Seasons are transitional unless you choose to allow the world to move around you while you stand still. But you are called to be more than stagnant. To be stagnant would be to deny the world the joy of your presence. Let the words of Billy Graham reassure you: "I have read the last page of the Bible. It's all going to turn out all right." I hope you find comfort in these words. What you are experiencing is nothing new to the human race. It has happened before, loss, betrayal, grief, addictions, death, life. Change is not new to humanity, just to you. *"History merely repeats itself. It has all been done before. Nothing under the sun is truly new"* (Ecclesiastes 1:9). Yes, it sucks to experience these life moments. Embrace the suck, acknowledge it, but please, dear loved one, do not dwell in it. This too shall pass. I understand the heartache is real and the pain cannot simply be pushed under the rug. I'm right there with you. But it can be surrendered to the throne room of God. Let's surrender the pain together.

Let us pray.

Dear God,

I surrender my season and life to you. I seek your love and comfort in each and every season as I try to make each harvest count for your kingdom and the call you have placed upon my life. I surrender all the pain of seasons past into your hands, God. Please deliver me from my pain and sorrow. Heal my heart and mind. Restore my joy for tomorrow. Fill me with your wisdom and discernment as I work my way closer to you. Thank you for loving me and guiding me as I walk with you in this new season. Protect my feet as I walk, Lord, and let no harm befall me as I seek your way in my life. Let all that has been stolen from me in seasons past be restored to me according to your perfect timing. I trust you, Lord, to be with me in each season of my life.

In Jesus' name I pray...

Amen

Exercise _____ ✎

Take a moment to reflect on what season you are in. Write about this season below and take a moment to list three to five positive moments of this season.

_____

_____

_____

_____

_____

_____

_____

_____

_____

_____

CHAPTER 2

DARING TO LIVE

"A time to be born and a time to die."

Ecclesiastes 3:2a

A NEED FOR SPEED

How fast do you have to be driving to crash and die? The pedal resisted being pressed to the floorboard. The speedometer was still climbing as my vision clouded. The stars twinkled as they observed my car speeding on the late December night as I drove home from the happiest place on earth. I was focused on the needle, trying to move it to the 100 mph mark. Hoping and believing that would be fast enough to end my life. The concrete barrier I had previously scouted was ahead, and I was determined to hit it, full speed. At 17, all I could think of was wanting the pain to end. As I propelled down the Osceola Parkway, my heart rate increased and I knew that this moment was a pivotal one. "Don't, it is not your time…" resonated in my ear as I prepared to yank the steering wheel.

And I snapped out of my intense focus of speeding and began to slow down.

As the speedometer slowly descended to 90 mph I inhaled a deep, life-giving breath. At 85 mph, a shaky breath out. At 80, the Saturn stopped shuddering. When the needle touched 75, the burning and tightening in my throat started to choke me. At 70 mph, the burning had crept up, causing my face to burn and my eyes to blur. At 65, months of unshed tears of pain, angst, and shame began to pour down my cheeks, dripping off my chin. As the memories of the heartbeat and the hopeful dreams of a bright future were shattered. I deeply mourned the loss of my first child and wanted nothing more than to die, to be with her. The comforting words reminding me it was not my time caused me to pivot. If I was not intended to die tonight, then I would make a life worth living so that the loss of my first child was not in vain.

LIVING FOR TOMORROW

It has been 22 years since I heard that comforting voice tell me it was not my time to go. The intensity of the peace and love that accompanied that tender voice was the thread I clung to when I doubted my ability to get back up after hard time. Nothing can prepare you for the loss of someone you love. Shattered dreams can leave our spirits crushed. I imagine this is how Jesus' disciples felt when they witnessed his death. Perhaps you have felt the agony of losing someone you love, perhaps you have not. Either way, the cycle of birth, life, and death is one that we cannot escape no matter how hard we try to avoid it. Death is inevitable. No one is exempt to this fact. Sometimes after a death, living seems unbearable. Somedays it takes every last ounce of energy and courage to wake up, get dressed, and then function in society as we are expected to do. Only to come home, get back in bed, and pray that tomorrow does not come so you do not have to repeat today. Life at this stage sucks. Embrace it. It will get better. I promise. Hang on.

The new day comes, whether we want it to or not. Mother Teresa once said, "Yesterday is gone. Tomorrow has not yet come. We have only today. Let us begin." So, my friend, begin with the life you have today. You have a choice to recognize that something about today is a gift from God, or you have the choice to throw that gift away. Those who struggle with asthma would tell you, just the fact that you can breathe without struggling is a gift. If that is the only one you can claim today, do it.

God gave life to man by breathing into his nostrils the breath of life (New American Standard Bible Genesis 2:7). Thankfulness and gratitude multiply in life and you will become pregnant with good thoughts and actions as you grow and heal. Your cup will soon overflow with joy, peace, and love as you focus on the smallest measures of these in your life. There are times in our lives that we are pregnant with ideas, dreams, and gifts that require labor, through physical and mental hard work, in order to bring forth new life. You carry within you a seed that was planted by God to be birthed at a specific time because you were created for a purpose (Jeremiah 1:5). A purpose that will give you a future and a hope (Jeremiah 29:11). Sometimes life throws us curveballs that seem to abort these dreams and ideas, but any seed planted by God will come to fruition if you water it, provide a safe and stable atmosphere, and allow it to grow.

When a woman is pregnant, doctors most often can detect new life as early as eight weeks by ultrasound. They seek the heartbeat as they scan her belly and determine how far along she is. Every pregnant woman will tell you in the last weeks of her pregnancy that she is ready for it to be over. She wants a healthy baby and she wants it out now. The load she is carrying has become heavy and difficult to carry. Jesus calls to us, *"Come to me, all who labor and are heavy laden, and I will give you rest."* (English Standard Version Matthew 11:28). The season of incubating is almost over and mama is ready for the next season, the new baby. Mama is ready for the harvest; her body has provided a nearly perfect environment for this baby to grow and thrive and it is time for it to be born To see, smell, and touch the fruit of her womb after diligently caring for the life within her. Patience is not an option; she had to simply sit and wait for the child to be ready to be birthed. She cannot rush the process. Doing so would be dangerous to the life and safety of baby and potentially mother. There is a knowing and a fear that the life within her has a purpose. Will she be able to be the mama this baby needs to grow and prosper into their own destiny? Will she be able to provide an environment that is rich in love, support, and provisions that will allow the child to thrive?

What are you pregnant with today that is growing inside of you? It is anger, bitterness or resentment, past betrayals, loss, and heartbreak? It is feeling unworthy of who you want to be? Please surrender that pain and heartache to Jesus, who loves you just as you are, and prepare to cultivate a new harvest of joy and love. Are you pregnant with joy, love, and abundance? Praise God! For now you can share that abundance with others to encourage them.

Pregnancy is a time of unseen growth. If you are pregnant with pain, you give birth to more pain. When you are pregnant with hope, you will give birth to more hope. You will see manifestation, the evidence of your pregnancy. There is evidence of the growth by the fullness of the belly. The details of the infant inside are yet unseen. This is just like faith. We cannot always see the evidence of our faith, like our babies growing inside, but you see the workings of faith as you grow in it.

With each one of my pregnancies, around the seventh month I was just over it. The cravings, the cramping, the twinges, rib kicks, breakouts, weird hair, all of it.

I wanted this season to be over. I was so uncomfortable in my own skin and unable to find relief that I was often irritable. I have to admit, I was impatient with the process, but I knew that rushing the process was not an option. When the baby is born early, lungs are underdeveloped. The heart is not fully functioning, kidneys cannot eliminate waste properly. *"Whatever is true, whatever is noble, whatever is right, whatever is pure, whatever is lovely, whatever is admirable--if anything is excellent or praiseworthy--think about such things"* Phillipians 4:8 NIV

When you are impatient with your own healing process and your heart is pushed too soon, and you are not healed from your trauma, you emerge from that dark season unprepared for life. There is a reason a healthy pregnancy takes so long: it allows for the proper development and growth for the birth of a healthy new life. Please know I am sensitive to pregnancies that are high risk and complicated. That is not at all what I am touching on here. Those unique situations also offer the opportunity to speak to your heart and bring freedom as well.

Just before going into labor, and sometimes during labor, fear creeps in. The mind starts to play tricks on you and the fear causes anxiety and doubt about the next phase. What happens after the pushing is over? Do not focus on the fear. Focus on the good in this moment, for this will alleviate your fear and anxiety. This will be the catalyst for a positive change in your life. *"Finally, brothers and sisters, whatever is true, whatever is noble, whatever is right, whatever is pure, whatever is lovely, whatever is admirable--if anything is excellent or praiseworthy--think about such things"* (New International Version, Phillipians 4:8)

My friend, think upon the birth of Jesus, the savior of the world. He was born in a manger, no fancy hospital, not even a nice little warming light to keep him toasty warm. No, he was born and placed in a feed trough for barn animals. Don't you think his mama must have wondered what next? Mary and Joseph were visited by great dignitaries bringing expensive gifts fit for a king, prophesying great miracles and wonders. And the word says, *"Mary treasured up all these things and pondered them with her heart."* (New International Version Luke 2:18). She literally pondered on the noble, right, pure, and lovely despite her surroundings and the political climate that dictated her newborn son be put to death.

The new season about to begin is filled with much potential. And as it arrives, the temptation to quit will be the strongest. When the load you have been carrying for so long begins to feel unbearable, that is when you most desire to put it down, but you can't because everything will fall apart. Perhaps that is your soul cry? I just cannot do this anymore, God, please help me? The burden of the season has become too heavy for you to carry? Maybe you are beyond fed up with the status quo of life and wish to quit and walk away. That, my friends, is the final pangs of labor. It is time to PUSH!

This final push is what matters the most. It is through the pain of that last push, that last painful moment of releasing the fear, doubt, and pain, that new life is born. This final push, the last leg of the marathon, is beckoning to be finished. Finish strong, don't quit, just finish strong. The winning is in the finishing. Continue to seek the Lord as you bear down to complete your current season. It will all be worth it in the end. Aborting the mission is not possible at this point. There is too much to lose. You were made to carry the load until the end. Focus. Your efforts are about to produce a life of such abundant joy that you will not be able to contain yourself, and your joy will be contagious to others. The rush of endorphins as you finish the labor is God's gift to alleviate the pain of childbirth. Yes, we must endure great hardship during the process, but relief comes, just like joy.

BIRTHING NEW LIFE

Your new life has eternal benefits with Christ; however, it does not come with a risk-free guarantee. What it does come with is an eternal life guarantee. This life and the struggles we face in each season are temporary. No struggle we face lasts forever. Think back to this day five years ago: do you remember what irritated you?

Who rubbed you wrong? What bill you were struggling to pay? I know for a fact I cannot remember those details, which is why it is so important to remember that when we feel overwhelmed by our struggles in life, we must capture our thoughts, and remember this too shall pass ... it is only temporary.

When I was having a mini pity party, I got caught up in the mess and lies of comparing my life to the lives of those around me. I saw their struggles and thought, "Oh my gosh, I could so handle that, why is she struggling with it when I could handle that so easily, and why are my struggles something I know she can deal with?" However, upon reflection I realized there is no growth in a life with no struggle. If life is without challenges, how do I grow and mature mentally, physically, and spiritually? Your character, faith, and endurance cannot be challenged if life is set to cruise control in every season.

It was during a difficult season when I read **_Everybody's Got Something_** by Robin Roberts. In it, she quotes her mother: *"If everyone threw their troubles into a pile and stood around and saw what each person was dealing with, we would each reach back in and take back what we put in."* I could not and did not see the day-to-day internal struggles my friends were facing. I saw only the exterior front that they released to me. Psalm 139:13 says, *"Certainly you made my mind and heart; you wove me together in my mother's womb."* (New English Bible). God knows your heart, he knows the number of hairs on your head, and your struggles in life are no surprise to him. He has already released the answer and healing to your trials. Life has meaning beyond the challenges and darkness you face today. The situations you are facing in this life are unique to you; they are designed to mold and shape your character, your faith, your mettle, your core being of who you were created to be. God has made no mistake in creating you and your life. It is time to stop doubting God and yourself and live a life of purpose.

LIFE DISRUPTED

Have you ever had a contingency plan for the "what if's" in life? Living a life of purpose means you have consciously thought to allow for the disruptions of life. Losing a loved one or a job, enduring a break up, seeing a hopeful dream shut down … these all lead to life disrupted. The painful experience of the death of a loved one is unavoidable. Too often we take for granted that we have tomorrow to finish the conversation or project only to find that tomorrow did not come for someone. Sadly, many only realize this after they lose someone they love dearly and then the lesson is learned and appreciated.

The disruption to our daily lives when we lose someone we love is shattering. I once had a friend ask me, *"Is there a right way to grieve?"* She had recently lost two uncles within a short period of time. I have learned through various means that there is no one right way to grieve the loss of someone you love. Who am I to say your process is right or wrong? What I can say, though, is that grief takes time in order to heal.

> *"Grief is the healing mechanism we have in order to deal with change"*
>
> Schneider & Zimmerman, 2006

Whether that loss is a job, move, diagnosis, etc., it takes its toll on even the most steadfast, faithful, and resilient. Grief challenges us to rely heavily on God's strength and not our own. It strengthens our faith and character over time, which requires us to rely on God for healing to overcome grief.

Living through loss, in all its shapes and sizes, is where you learn that a time to be born and a time to die is more than a cliché. It is where you learn how to live despite the pain. It is learning to live with joy in exchange for sorrow. The fruit of your womb depends on how you heal from grief when one season ends and another has not yet begun.

The Lord is near to the broken-hearted and saves the crushed in spirit (Psalm 34:18). Even Jesus knew grief as he wept at the loss of a great friend who he loved (John 11:35). He truly understands your heart pain. And his desire is to meet us where we are dead and broken. In the same chapter Jesus asks to be led to where his dead friend laid in a tomb (John 11:33) and it was there, once he was by his friend's side, that he called to his friend to come out of the tomb and live. My friend, Jesus is coming to you, and calling you out of your dead space. He is calling you back to life.

Whatever had to end, had to, just as the seasons have to change to accommodate the next stage of life. Some things must stop to allow new things to exist. New schedules, jobs, and relationships, cannot be mixed with the old. New wine cannot go into an old wine skin because it will destroy the new vessel. It does not mean that anything was wrong with what had ended; it means simply that the purpose and vessel of that time has ended, and a new season, new life, has to form so you may fulfill your destiny.

So, how do you cultivate your light in the season of life and death? You focus on what is good, true, pure, and lovely. God will send you gifts such as these, known only to you for they are that unique. You will know beyond a shadow of a doubt that God sent these gifts to answer your heart cry for hope by the peace that surrounds you when you decide to allow him into your heart. His provision will be so specifically packaged for you that you will not be able to say it was anyone else but God who sent this gift. Let us activate this gift through prayer.

Dear God,

Your word says to give thanks in all things. So, here I am, Lord, giving you thanks for all that I have experienced up until this moment in my life. I thank you for each and every season, situation and challenge I face. I trust you, Lord, to bring me through it to the other side, whole, prosperous, and healed. I may not understand this season of life and death right now, but I trust you. I trust you to help me understand your heart in this matter as I grow and develop in this season. I trust you with my life, Lord. I trust you with all that I am pregnant with. I trust that at the right time and place, I will give birth to new seasons of abundant life: healthy and whole. Full of joy and laughter. You will trade my sorrows for joy and I will dance like David in gratitude and joy. You, Lord, are my strength and refuge, my help in ever-present trouble. No weapon formed against me shall prosper all the days of my life. Help me, God, strengthen me as I labor and make the final push into my new season with you.

In Jesus' name I pray...

Amen

Exercise _____

*List all the good, true, pure and lovely parts of your life.
Focus on these as you pray over them.*

_____

_____

_____

_____

_____

_____

_____

_____

_____

_____

CHAPTER 3

PLANTING A NEW SEASON

"A time to plant and a time to uproot."

Ecclesiastes 3:2b

PREPARING THE SOIL

Is that a pretty weed, or a tender budding shoot of a sunflower? Day 47 of this stay–at-home order has me questioning what I planted three weeks ago. I struggle to remember what I even planted, and now what do I do with the green stem jutting out of the dark soil? Or, better yet, um, where the heck are the green stems?

Like many people, my family built a planter box and planted a variety of seeds to prepare for a lack of produce in the market. We thought it would save some cash, and really, give us something extra do to with our time while at home during the stay at home order. Staring at the small garden bed I wondered, "What will I be harvesting when all of this is said and done?" What will I uproot to make compost with, and what will I keep, to nurture and enjoy? During this time of great reflection, awakening, planting, and harvesting, hope wraps its tendrils around my heart and I can see is evidence that something was planted in some rows, but in others, nothing. There is indeed a season of planting and uprooting … but what, I wondered, do we do while we wait?

Building the planter box, the home of our new garden, was exciting stuff. The kids were excited to help and were joyful with anticipation of what would come from it. Filling the box with soil, we ended up covered in fine particles of dirt, fertilizer, and who knows what else. As the kids followed the instructions of planting the seeds in rows, spaced out appropriately, their faces were alight with joy. As I watched, I wondered, "Is this how you feel, God, when we go about your business?" Each day since the planting we have diligently watered the garden, and after about ten days we started searching for signs of life within the dark bed of soil. And I started to become anxious. What if the seeds were bad and don't grow? Was the soil appropriate for what we planted? What if we did not provide the seeds with the proper soil, sunlight, or water to grow?

Wendell Berry says, *"The soil is the great connector of lives, the source and destination of all. It is the healer and restorer, and by which disease passes into health, age into youth, and death into life. Without proper care for it we can have no community, because without proper care for it we can have no life."* (Berry, 1996) Jesus also says this when he gives a parable of the farmer scattering his seeds (Mark 4:3-8). Jesus was speaking not only of plants, but of hearts. Words that we speak are like the planting of seeds, to our own hearts and to the hearts of others. Out of our mouths we speak life or death. In Proverbs 4:23, we are cautioned to plant our words wisely: *"Above all else, guard your heart, for everything you do flows from it."* The condition of our hearts affects the harvest of the life that we live. When we live with hardened hearts, nothing grows from it and in fact, the seeds placed there will be eaten up by life (Mark 4:4).

When our hearts are soft but shallow , the seeds grow just a bit; but because the roots cannot get down deep, the storms of life will cause that plant to die quickly (Mark 4:5). The seed planted in a hostile environment cannot grow; it is choked out by the pain, anger and animosity that surrounds it, and this unhealed heart cannot produce fruit (Mark 4:7). The seed planted in fertile, healthy soil is able to grow and flourish, producing fruit not only for the farmer, but the farmer's family, community, and nation. The seeds—the words—you plant in your heart are what produce the harvest, but the heart, the soil, must be softened and healthy to have the best possible outcome. *"Nothing is more appealing than speaking beautiful, life giving words. For they release sweetness to our souls and inner healing to our spirits."* (Proverbs 16:24).

I pray you take a moment and do a heart check. Check to see how your heart is doing. There is no shame, no blame, and no judgment on your current heart posture. It has endured life and struggle and pain. There are places that need tending to, but that does not mean it is ruined. You have overcome betrayal, just like Jesus. You have overcome greed and loss; hold your head up, dear sister. You are not done yet. Your garden has been planted long ago by God. This is the waiting period where you submit yourself to God and allow your heart to bloom with grace. Where life plants you, bloom with grace. Allow God to turn your mess into your message to the world. Allow him to turn that barren garden box into a blooming array of color, ready for the harvest. The joy of your heart, the hope planted deep inside you at your conception, will grow. Are you ready to soften yourself to allow God to gently tend to you, his precious daughter?

This softening is not easy, trust me, I know. The more you resist, the harder it becomes to allow Him in. But, when He enters into your heart, you are beautifully humbled. You may be there now, on your knees, ready for his work to begin. Perfect. You are exactly where you need to be in order to tend to your garden. Ready for the toiling of the soil. Do not worry about what others will say about your planting and growing process; it is not theirs to go through. But later, you will be able to share your harvest with others who have harvested their gardens. You will be able to enjoy the hearts and fruits of others who have done the work as you have. Sister, your healing is about to impact future generations. It is bigger than you and your immediate family and friends. This is about generations of people seeking abundant hope and life. Hundreds of thousands will be healed of pain and sorrow because of your groundbreaking transformation of the heart. Proverbs 18:21 says, *"The tongue has the power of life and death, and those who love it will eat its fruit."* Those who have hope and love in their hearts, speak love and hope. Those who have pain and death in their hearts, speak to that pain. Which do you want to plant?

PLANTING THE SEEDS

Merriam-Webster Dictionary defines plant/sow the seeds as:

1. To cause (an idea, feeling, etc.) to be in someone's mind
2. To create a situation in which (something) is likely or certain to happen or develop (Merriam-Webster, n.d.)

I promise you, you are not even aware of the impact you have on those around you. Simply by being your unique, authentic self, you have already begun to plant seeds of hope in others. Even on the days you feel completely lost, vulnerable, and shattered, someone watches you in wonder and amazement at your strength, grace, and tenacity. So, my friend, what seeds—what thoughts—have you allowed others to plant in your mind? Are they seeds of empowerment or are they seeds of discouragement, condemnation, and sarcasm? Those ugly seeds of discord, ones that cause you to doubt your beauty, they need to go, sis. Those seeds, those weeds that grew from those words, need to be uprooted. They are choking out the good harvest all around you. You are too important to allow unnecessary seeds to grow.

If you question which thoughts to get rid of, let me get real and specific. The lies of the devil that say to you, "you are not enough, you are too shy, ugly, inexperienced, unworthy," those thoughts or anything in alignment with those thoughts are weeds that do not belong in your garden. Get rid of them! Uproot them and throw them in the compost bin, the fire pit, whatever you have to do. Grasp those thoughts as they enter your mind—make sure you get the roots too—and throw it away. It's trash, garbage, it does not help your garden grow. They do not soften your soil or bring a good harvest. These ugly thoughts are designed to slow and stop your growth and abort your harvest. No one can farm the garden of your heart for you. No one is going to uproot the nasty from your garden for you. This is where the toiling gets hard, sis. Embrace the suck and just do it. Do it for your future, and the ones you love. They are depending on you to embrace the suck by example and do the work necessary for a garden to grow in righteous spender and glory. This season of toiling is temporary and oh so worth it. The seeds planted inside of you, by God, are too important to be left neglected and choked out by weeds. King David started his life as a shepherd boy, but the seed that God planted inside of him was that of a king! God planted specific seeds inside of you that he wants you to cultivate and nurture with a harvest that will supersede what man says can grow from you.

TIMING IS EVERYTHING

Planting the wrong seed at the wrong time will not result in the desired harvest. In fact, you may receive no harvest if you try to force the planting before its proper time or place. Being mindful in prayer to seek the Lord for his timing of planting is critical for the best harvest possible. If you are blessed to live in a climate where almost anything can grow, then you are truly blessed with a healthy environment.

Even the best environment has soil conditions that must be tended to. However, most people live in an environment that requires hard work and dedication. You have to plan according to location of the garden, climate, soil conditions, water restrictions, etc. This aligns with our heart conditions. Some of us have more trauma to heal from than others. Some of us need deliverance in ways others don't. And sis, there is no criticism or judgment in how much work you have to do to get that harvest.

You may need to borrow tools from your neighbors. You may need a trusted mentor or two to help you through the process. These tools, mentors, can provide you with prayer, laughter, guidance, and resources you need in order to grow. Do not be afraid to ask for the help, sis. James 4:2-3 corrects us when we say we do not have x, y, z because we have not asked for x, y, z and maybe we did, but with the wrong motive. So, in truth and love, I am asking you to check your heart, check your motive and ask God for what you need in order to grow in hope and love. These mentors and the tools you receive will require you to work hard to get through the hard labor of working your garden. You must take the time to be focused, strategic, diligent, and disciplined in taking care of yourself when you are facing a less than perfect environment in which to garden.

When you speak to other farmers (your mentors) and borrow their tools (wisdom and insight), you gain knowledge that will increase your storehouse, always for the benefit of not only yourself, but others. You get to share with others the gifts God has planted within you! When you do, you are able to help others who are tending to their gardens as well. This creates sustainability of the heart and soul. Those who are like-minded with you, planting, sowing, and reaping will grow alongside you. They, too, are being sharpened by borrowing your tools, just as in Proverbs 27:17 (NIV), *"As iron sharpens iron, so one person sharpens another."*

No matter what you planted last year, with the wrong climate and soil, if you have not watered your crops, they will wither up and die. Just like my New Year's resolution to lose fifteen pounds. When you set your mind on a goal, but then do not give yourself the benchmarks or tools to reach the goals, they are left unmet. The right measure of water is critical to whether or not life blooms or a drowning ensues. Jesus tells us that whoever believes in him, will have rivers of living water within them (John 7:38).

Thus, when we allow Jesus into our gardens, he will provide us with the food and water necessary for our gardens to be healed, refreshed, and life-giving. The garden can only sustain itself for so long before the soil must rest and be renewed. Farmers use this tactic when they rotate fields during different planting seasons. It is a form of sustainable farming that allows the soil to heal and prepare for the next planting season. The farmer understands the soil, just as Jesus understands your heart. He knows exactly what healing you need in order to be ready for the next planting season. If you are in a season of rest, rest easy, sister, for this time is temporary and it too shall pass.

Understanding the season of rest and boundaries is important for garden growth. Perimeters, like a planter box, are useful in keeping not only weeds at bay, but pests too. You know those pesky distractions and annoyances that seem innocent at first but then choke the life out of you? Or is that only me? A boundary is necessary when growing valuable crops, sister. Sometimes you have to use tools like pesticide to keep the bugs away, but do what you have to do. Do not allow the devil, his delusions, distractions, or devastation into your garden to keep you from growing. Be bold and grow anyway. Use the tools given to you in the world by your mentors and keep growing, cultivating, and waiting patiently for your harvest.

These delusions, distractions, or devastations need to be identified and taken out. In keeping it real with you, what is growing in your life that does not belong? Is it a relationship that needs to end? A job that has nothing to do with the dream burning in your heart? What behavior are you covering up that defies the treasure you truly are? My friend, whatever it is, that is the weed you need to pull out of your garden. And you will need to monitor your garden continually for new weeds that may spring up. You will think you have it under control and BAM! Right next to your prized plant will be a nasty weed, ready to choke out your future harvest.

Sometimes these weeds are weeds of comparison. Forgive us, God. Sometimes we start projects or jobs because we see someone else has what we want. Covetousness is not cute. In fact, that would be a weed in your garden and in reality that could someone else's prized plant. Weeds represent actions, behaviors, persons, jobs, houses, cars that simply do not belong in our lives right now. It is a risk to your future joy, healing, and harvest. And sometimes they look like good things, and they are good things. Dandelions are a great example. They are pretty, and edible, and medicinal, but they are a nuisance in your yard. Do you need them in your garden if they are stealing valuable nutrients and water from what you planted?

PREPARING THE HARVEST

This is your opportunity to be honest with yourself. This is not a pleasant process; often it is painful and it is necessary. It may require hard conversations. You may need to fill the gap left behind. You may need to sit and heal in silence for a bit. Devote yourself to activities that will help you grow the garden you want and have envisioned for yourself. All that time and energy you spent focusing on the weeds can now be directed toward the purpose--driven life you were created to live. Do not worry about the weeds starving; remember, they belong in a different garden. When you cut out the weeds you get rid of despair, pain, doubt, fear, discouragement, shame, guilt, distractions, and accusations. You make room to receive love, mercy, forgiveness, joy, grace, hope, inspiration, peace, and comfort. These, my sweet sister, are your harvests to come. They are yours to capture up in your cheerful garden basket and share at the dinner table, surrounded by your friends and family who love, honor, and cherish you.

Now, is the time, girl! You have done the physical and soul-wrenching work of tending your garden. You have planted, watered, and weeded it. You have waited while your garden prospered. It is now time to collect the bounty of all that you have sown.

Harvest time is here; it is a time of celebration and joy! There is a reason we have Thanksgiving every year. It started in 1621 when the pilgrims celebrated their successful wheat crop and overflowing store cupboards with a three-day feast. Sisters, 2020 has had me on a 57-day feast. My pants tell me the truth; I am blessed. There was so much bounty to be had in 1621 that the people sat and ate for three days straight in fellowship with each other. Do you see that the harvest overflowed for them because of their faithful trust in the process of seed, time, and harvest? Yes, there were periods of scant, scarcity, and concern, but the harvest came after diligent caring for the soil and crops! Similar Thanksgiving harvests are observed around the world in appreciation of the abundance of a harvest. From flower festivals in Portugal to the fruit fairs of Thailand, these celebrations of harvest commemorate the bounty and abundance of a good growing season. Every crop yields a harvest in its own season and time. Some are summer season festivals, others winter or spring, each with its own unique purpose to honor that which was so hard to curate and cultivate during the growing season. Each farmer tending their crops, faithfully trusting the process, knowing that in due time, they will see the reward of their hard work. Just as Paul encourages us in Galatians, *"Let us now grow weary of doing good, for in due season we will reap if we do not give up."* (6:9).

"As long as the earth endures, seedtime and harvest, cold and heat, summer and winter, day and night will

never cease." (Genesis 8:22 NIV). Just as the transitions of seasons never change, neither does God's love for you. His love never fails, never gives up, and never abandons us. I want to challenge you to pray this prayer and seek quiet time alone to meditate on the love of God. This loving faithfulness He covers us with is what will guide you through your season of planting and uprooting. With each stage of transformation, His loving presence will cover you. Embrace it and treasure it; it is the substance that will sustain you through the longest of droughts. If God can make a rock provide water to the Israelites as they travel (Exodus 17:6) what more will he do for you when you seek him for relief from your drought?

Let us pray.

Father God,

I want to thank you for the seasons of change. I thank you for the opportunity to plant and uproot in my life. I pray for your guidance and wisdom to plant, in good soil, the seeds of hope, love, and prosperity. I thank you for providing me to proper tools to tend to the garden you have given me. Father, I ask you to help me identify weeds I have allowed into my garden that are blocking my harvest. Strengthen and sustain me as I remove those weeds so that I may have the freedom to grow in your holy presence. Thank you for the rains that will refresh the fields and not flood them. For the sunlight of your love that will draw the plants from the soil towards your heavenly dwelling.

Thank you for the purity of the harvest that will not suffer due to famine, flood, or drought.

God, please remove all of the impurities of my heart so that I can properly grow, sustain and harvest all that you have already supplied to me in my mother's womb. I decree and declare that the crops that planted today create harvests that will bless future generations.

In Jesus' name I pray...

Amen

Exercise

Identify seeds you need to plant and tend to in your life. Identify the weeds in your life that need to be uprooted. Pray for God to strengthen you as you seek to remove the unnecessary plants in your garden.

_____

_____

_____

_____

_____

_____

_____

_____

CHAPTER 4

HEALING IN YOUR SEASON

"A time to kill and a time to heal."

Ecclesiastes 3:2a

KILLING TIME

As my head settles into the pillow, the blue light in the dark room glows tauntingly; it is already 11 p.m. Thoughts pop up in my brain as I try to sleep. I forgot to switch over the laundry. Crap … Carson kept to himself a lot today. He seemed extra quiet. Mental note, less chores tomorrow, and spend more time with him. Khloe seemed to be extra whiny today. Did she eat enough protein? Was she not challenged enough today? Or maybe she was stressed from too much activity. I wonder if Keola is taking care of himself. God, I'm so worried about this grown man-child. Have we done enough as parents? Did we raise him right? Is he making strong choices when we are not around? God, I'm not ready for him to move out; I'm not really sure if HE's ready to move out. But he's determined. Oh Lord, help us! I feel like I wasted a lot of time today. How important is a completely organized house if everyone is unhappy? Help me, Jesus, to hear you better tomorrow. Kevin, he seemed to need me a little more today too; mental note, schedule the kids to go to Grandma's so we can have a date night.

Am I the only woman to have these types of thoughts as she falls asleep? Maybe yours weren't about your children, but about your job or your relationship with a loved one. Have you had those days, where tiny prayers end with a snore because exhaustion from a day of living life kicks in? Wondering if I was a good enough wife, mom, daughter, sister, friend to those around me. To be honest, I don't have a consistent schedule of making sure I use my time wisely. Some days, I kill a lot of time doing absolutely nothing worthwhile, and in the meantime, my to-do list grows. Other days, I slay all day, tackling one thing after another, getting a lot done, but wondering if I gave my family enough of me. I believe God wants us to live balanced lives, so where, God, does the scale balance in my life?

All throughout Ecclesiastes 3:1-8, I noticed a pattern. There is a balancing of scales. There is life and death, good and evil. It begs the question if there is a time to kill, then, are we are also given a time to heal? I am not here to tell you about God and killing, nor am I about to go into murder versus killing. But, what I do want to chat about is how if there is a time to kill, we are given time to heal. And sometimes, that killing is not of human life, but of time, resources, relationships, etc. God then intended for us to heal from that pain. Sister, you are a treasure, and made in the very image of God. I trust that if God says it's time to kill, it's time for war. So, who on earth are we at war with?

SLAYING THE GIANT

Spiritual warfare is that timeless fight between good and evil. It does not exist only for the super religious. Those who attempt to surrender to what is best for their lives will encounter a spiritual enemy designed specifically for them, to stop them in their tracks. This spiritual enemy, for the sake of imagery, could be a giant, as in Goliath. Identifying the giant would be the first step for trying to take him down. Every military power in the history of mankind has sent out scouts and spies to understand their enemies. Knowing who they are, how they move, what makes them tick is necessary to defeat them. Knowing the strategy of your giant, your spiritual enemy, is critical for outsmarting him and defeating him. Take the battle between David and Goliath: David used a rock, a weapon that seems so simple. Yet in this case it was genius. Goliath was too big for David to take down in hand–to-hand combat. Because David had experience executing wild animals to protect his sheep out in the wild, he knew what he COULD do to win the battle against an enemy larger than himself.

When we face our own enemies, we do not battle with flesh and blood, but with the spirit. Because you know

God, because you believe in Jesus, your battles are no longer of this world, but of a spiritual world. You see, Goliath was sent to intimidate and stop David from succeeding and becoming a KING. His battle was not a simple battle for territory; oh no, it was for a godly inheritance. It was for future generations to be blessed by God. Goliath represents the spiritual forces working against you to stop you from your rightful inheritance. 2 Corinthians 10:3-5 (New Living Translation) says, *"We are human, but we don't wage war as humans do. We use God's mighty weapons, not worldly weapons, to knock down the strongholds of human reasoning and to destroy false arguments."*

So, my friend. What giant are you facing that challenges your inheritance? Who hurt you? Who or what broke your spirit? What relationship is so difficult it challenges you? What addiction have you battled? What event caused your entire world to shift so that now you feel that you have no foundation on which to stand? What fear are you standing in the valley with today? How is he taunting you? What addiction is calling your name? Is he calling you by your sin? By your shame? Is he trying to define your character by your past mistakes? My friend, I am here with you, crying with you, because the torment of being shamed, blamed, called out on our ugly in condemnation is painful! More importantly, Jesus is right beside you as you face these painful thoughts. I bring you a better message. One of good news! One that defeats the giant you are facing.

My sister, you are fearfully and wonderfully made. You are redeemed and justified (Romans 3:24), you are free (Romans 6:6) of all condemnation (Romans 8:1), you are accepted by Christ (Romans 15:7), you are chosen, holy, and blameless before God (Ephesians 1:4), you are forgiven by the grace of God (Ephesians 1:7). Sister, you are of a royal priesthood. No weapon formed against you shall prosper. You are equipped to kill every enemy that comes against who you are in Christ. Are you ready to slay the giant standing in front of you? No one can do it for you. Now is the time for you to stand tall. It is time for you to lift your head up, child. It is time for you to rise up from the ashes. You are not done. Your future has not been aborted. Your calling is still waiting for you; it is right there, on the other side of the valley. Just behind the giant is your promised land. Come on, sis, you've got this. Your boots are dirty from traveling, planting, and harvesting. That's OK. They are proof of your journey being filled with signs and wonders from heaven above. Plant your feet, pick up your slingshot. Place the rock in the sling, take your aim. And now, inhale. As you exhale, release the pain of the past as you relax the tension of the slingshot and let it fly. Now, repeat after me: "I am chosen, forgiven, redeemed, healed, blameless, fearfully and wonderfully made. No weapon formed against me shall prosper. What the devil intended for evil, God intended for good. God is doing a new thing in my life."

You are made new, set free from sin and shame. This new thing is your healed journey in a life of freedom. The price has been paid on your debt. He was killed so you could be healed. The word says, for by HIS stripes that you were healed (1 Peter 2:24). God promised us a healing long before we were ever born. The journey we each take is different. Your sisters in your inner circle need you. The friends you have yet to make need you too. They need your light to shine as a beacon of hope. The road that travels between killing the giant and being healed is not the same for everyone. Make sure you give yourself some grace, mercy and forgiveness as you travel towards your healing in the promised land.

WALKING TOWARD HEALING

Walking toward healing will require consistent effort even when you do not feel like it. The commitment you make to healing guarantees you will reach your desired destination. Some days you will run, others you will crawl and others you will simply lie there because you are too exhausted to move. I get it. You must surrender as you work toward healing. You must surrender to the will of God even when you don't understand all His plans and processes. Trust in His word that He is nursing your soul's wounds as you walk. He is restoring you back to health as you take baby steps to trust in Him. Psalm 41:3 (NLT) says, *"The Lord nurses them when they are sick and restores them to health."*

He is right beside you, taking good care of you. You have nothing to fear.

The old has passed away. Remember! Goliath WAS defeated. All your sins have been overcome. After the death of your spiritual enemy, healing begins. Psalm 103:3 (NLT) says, *"He forgives all my sins and heals all my diseases."* The diseases of your heart are the effects of sin found in pain, anger, pride, shame, and doubt. It is critical at this moment to fix your eyes on your creator: Matthew 6:22 (NLT) says, *"Your eye is like a lamp that provides light for your body. When your eye is healthy, your whole body is filled with light."* What are you fixing your eyes on as you walk toward your healing? If you are looking back, you cannot see where you are going. You are too focused on what is in the past to move forward without stumbling. To move forward without stumbling, you must look up. Look toward the horizon.

I used to ride horses competitively. My favorite area of competition was jumping. The thrill of coasting over the jump as your horse works hard to carry you safely over it is unlike anything else. It was during lessons that my riding instructor would call out to me, *"LOOK UP! When you look down as you go over the jump, you will go where your eyes go! If you don't want to fall, look up!"* And this is a mindset that has stuck with me whenever I have felt insecure or in pain about a situation or season of life.

This is just as true in our walk toward healing with God. If we rehearse the events and conversations that were so painful over and over again, we cannot move forward. We end up stuck. Remember the story of Lot and his wife? As they fled from Sodom they were instructed to not look back. As they fled the city, the wife looked back and was turned into a pillar of salt.

You know what salt does? It preserves. It dries food. It draws the water out. Do not allow your past to be preserved when you have growth and abundance assigned to you. Your pain was an experience, not a preservative.

Forgiveness lies between hurt and healed. *"Forgiving a person who has wronged you is never easy, but dwelling on those events and reliving them over and over can fill your mind with negative thoughts and suppressed anger,"* says Dr. Tyler VanderWeele, co-director of the Initiative on Health, Religion, and Spirituality at the Harvard T.H. Chan School of Public Health. *"Yet, when you learn to forgive, you are no longer trapped by the past actions of others and can finally feel free."* (VanderWheel, 2019)

You need to get deliberate about your healing to move forward. It is just like the woman who was so desperate for a healing touch from Jesus. She moved through a crushing crowd of people to just touch the hem of the garment of Jesus, knowing, *"If I can just touch his robe, I will be healed"* (Matthew 9:21NLT).

Keep your eyes forward. If you are not ready to lift your head up high, just raise your eyes. Sis, it is so hard to raise your eyes when you feel defeated. I understand this, truly. It sucks. Embrace the suck and look up. Look three feet in front of you. Focus on the next three steps. As you travel, raise your gaze every few miles. Look farther in front of you. You will begin to see the beautiful landscape that you are traveling. You will begin to see the beauty that surrounds you. The good people who travel the road with you will begin to be familiar. The path will begin to be comforting. Yes, challenges will arise, and you were created to overcome them.

TIPPING THE SCALES

The weight of the pain that killed you has been far too heavy. It is a burden you have been carrying for far too long. It is time to put it down and allow the scales to tip in your favor. It is time to realize that the season of killing is over. The season for healing has begun. You are walking into a season of abundance. The spiritual battle you have been fighting is already won. You are already victorious; your enemy has already been defeated. Now it is your time to walk out your healing. As you go, be sure to look up toward the horizon. Allow yourself to find your rhythm; don't try to rush today and suffer tomorrow. Healing takes time. No one person's healing is better or worse because of timing. It takes effort on your part to surrender to God for your healing;, he will take care of the rest.

Let us pray.

Heavenly Father,

You have given me a promise that there is a season to kill and a season to heal. I trust you to help me see the enemy and his plan to stop me from following you. I cast all of the stress, fear, pain, and trauma unto your shoulders, for the burden is heavy for me, but light for you. Forgive me, Lord, for trying to carry the burdens of pain and shame instead of surrendering it to you. I forgive those who have taxed my soul and have hurt my heart to the point of coping to get by and not healing. I forgive myself for trying to do it all in my own strength without forgiving others. I release all shame and blame, and I accept your love, grace, mercy, and forgiveness in exchange. I trade in my sorrow for joy with you here and now, Lord. Protect me from all negativity, demonic strongholds, soul ties, and associations that will distract me from you. I am covered by the armor of God, surrounded by the brilliant white light of Jesus. May there be a mirror of heavenly light to repel all attacks of negativity and the enemy. I dwell in the shelter of the almighty God, protected safe, and secure. I am whole, released from the shackles of pain, abuse, trauma, shame, and neglect. I am made new from this day forward. I forgive those who have hurt, taunted, and tormented me. My spirit is no longer tormented by the spiritual enemy that seeks to hurt me. I release all of my doubt and pride at your feet. In exchange I pick up my true identity in you.

As your child, I claim my birthright of healing. I am here to declare that I am healed by the blood of Jesus. I am worthy of your love which covers all of my sins. You alone are worthy of all praise, God.

In Jesus' name I pray...

Amen

Exercise _____ ✎

Who can you forgive? Get deliberate about choosing to forgive them. List those whom you need to forgive below. Once you have completed this step, get deliberate about moving forward with a lighter heart focused on your healing. List three ways you can do so starting today.

_____

_____

_____

_____

_____

_____

_____

_____

CHAPTER 5

CREATE SOMETHING NEW

"A time to tear down and a time to build."

Ecclesiastes 3:2b

BUILDING UP OR DOWN?

As you can see by now, the process of seasons is about a spiritual warfare on our minds. You will win this battle. You are the victor. You have identified what needs to be killed and weeded out of your garden. Now that you know what you have to eliminate, you can tear down the strongholds that have imprisoned you. A stronghold is a fortified place to protect against an attack. A castle, fortress, or bunker would be considered a stronghold. As we live life, we build up strongholds in our mind and heart to block out painful memories, people, or events. Strongholds are old, difficult, and discouraging challenges. They are trapped in you inner prison and challenge you throughout your life. Imagine that people are walking around bound up in these strongholds. Seemingly free, but truly prisoners of their minds. Ecclesiastes 3:2 reminds us that we have a prisoner stuck in the stronghold who needs to be let out.

A stronghold that is healthy is the stronghold of the Lord. Psalm 9:9 says, *"The Lord also will be a stronghold for the oppressed, a stronghold in times of trouble."* The Lord is the stronghold, the safe place, we run to in times of trouble. When this scripture was written, various skirmishes and wars were breaking out across the land. And sometimes the only place to run was to war and pray to God for safety. And he provided it. David acknowledges his protection in Psalm 144:2, where he declares, *"The Lord is my stronghold and my deliverer."* Maybe you are in the season of tearing down at the end of a season. This must be done to begin rebuilding your new life, a new season. For such a time as this.

TEARING DOWN THE STRONGHOLDS

All of my life the lie that weaved its way through each season was that I was not enough. It started when I was a young girl, and this thread of thought was subtly woven into every action I made. So I tried hard to be the good girl. I tried so hard to stay out of trouble, to earn praise. And when it backfired, I would isolate. It was a subconscious way of living that cycled for far too long. I did not realize what I needed to address until I had a crisis so severe that I could not get through a day without the elephant of anxiety on my chest. I was on the verge of a panic attack every moment of every day. I had spun so far out of control trying to please everyone around me that I had created chaos in my own life; something I swore I would never do.

In my desire to be found worthy and good enough, I made decisions that were detrimental to my faith, myself, family, and friends. I, the Christian woman who studied the Bible in college … fell hard. There was no relationship that was untouched by the pain and the lies of the stronghold on my life. It was then I realized just how strategic the strongholds on our mind can be. In unveiling my own pride, I realized my personal foundation was damaged and it was obvious that I had to start anew. I was given a choice by God to rebuild my life or truly allow the destruction to take over. I was at the transition point of a season. I had to surrender. There was no real choice for me; the only choice I wanted to make was to rebuild my life in faith on a new foundation. This required tearing down strongholds before I could even begin the process of rebuilding. My new foundation had to be rock solid. There could be no cracks in it. It had to be rebuilt; it had to be rebuilt with only the help of Jesus. He had to be my cornerstone for my new foundation.

"For no one can lay any foundation other than the one already laid, which is Jesus Christ"

1 Corinthians 3:11 NIV

LAYING THE FOUNDATION

In preparation for my new foundation, the ground had to be prepared. Preparing the foundation is just as fundamental when planting the garden. If you have never planted or never built, have you ever cooked? What did you start with? A recipe! This is your foundation. Whatever project you have ever started, it all began with a foundation. Just because you haven't built a home or planted a garden does not mean you have never laid a foundation of some sort. Your foundation and building may look different. God created us all to be unique. Do not be put off if these examples do not fit your life; think of one instance where you started from scratch and reflect on the foundation you had to lay to complete the task.

It was while I was in the season of tearing down that I came across 1 Peter 2:7, which says, *"Now, to you who believe, this stone is precious. But to those who do not believe, 'The stone which the builders rejected, this became the very cornerstone.'"* This stone is precious, but there will be those who do not recognize its value. The cornerstone was used in biblical times to mark the corner of the building; it guided workers as they built, providing a point of reference. It was usually the largest and most solid and carefully constructed part of the build. It was strategic in building a strong foundation. A weak cornerstone would make for a weak and unsafe building. For our purposes, recognizing Jesus as our standard of measurement and alignment is how to rebuild in our season. He is the foundation of your hope for this season.

Jesus, precious and beloved by God as His son, knew betrayal and rejection. Of His 12 closest friends, three rejected him as he was cruelly tortured and crucified as a criminal. His innocence was not enough to get those in his closest circle to be more than fair-weather friends. Life was great for the disciples while he was traveling, speaking to thousands, riding on his miraculous fame. But when trouble came to their door, they cut and ran. C'mon, can you imagine how heartbreaking this would have been? Ever had a friend or loved one at your side for years and then that person betrays you? Girl, that is reality for far too many of us. That heartache is relatable to Jesus. It made me realize that Jesus truly knows this pain of betrayal and he wants us to come to him with that pain. Lay it down at his feet and let him wrap his arms around you in comfort. God knows how the story ends. You are just beginning; this is not the end.

Because Jesus is such a gentleman, he will never force himself past our outer gates, our lives, to help us. This is where in our rebuilding we must seek him and invite him to come into our hearts to sit with us. Allow him to lead you as you rebuild. Check in with him as you would a contractor. Use him as your cornerstone in this season. Sometimes rebuilding has to be done in the midst of a storm. If this is you, I pray he calms your storm here and now. May his peace and love cover you as you sit in his presence. May forgiveness begin to flood your heart, for those who have hurt you, and for yourself. You are more than enough. You are worthy. He has enough love for all of us, no matter what you've done. Let him love you and be sure to show grace to yourself.

Someone is watching how you tear down and begin to rebuild your life. There are loved ones in your corner, silently watching you, waiting to see how you come out of it. They watch in wonder of your courageous spirit. Billy Graham once said, *"Courage is contagious: when a brave man takes a stand, the spines of others are stiffened."* As you lay your new foundation, what principles and values are you planning to stand on? The life you are building on needs a firm foundation. I love this quote from Anne Wojcicki: *"The reality is that the only way change comes is when you lead by example."* (Parrish, 2016) Is your current foundation strong enough to save your loved ones? Is it strong enough to hold everyone without collapsing? Mine wasn't. It had to be torn down and rebuilt with my trust in God and not myself this time. God himself tells us that we can trust him over and over; that he is a sure foundation (Isaiah 28:16).

PUTTING UP WALLS

Now that your foundation is solid, the real building can begin. The walls, plumbing, electrical, insulation, windows, and doors all need to be installed into this new home. Your new life has begun to take shape. While the time dragged as you were preparing and laying the foundation, time begins to go quickly as progress takes shape. The change in your heart becomes visible to those around you. Speaking bluntly here, people will let go of you as you build and change. Let them go. Insulate your walls to keep the heat from the presence of the Lord in, and the chill of the world out.

A few years ago I got aggressive with our home refresh and decided that our walls needed new drywall. I had no idea of the mess that was ahead of me. My poor husband. In the process of installing and finishing drywall I watched the tradesmen mud and tape the boards and I had a realization that brought me to tears: It takes a truly skilled person to not just install but also tape, mud, and sand the pieces together for a smooth wall. God is not asking for perfection on our part during this part of our rebuilding. He is asking you to hand him your pain, for it is His love that is the tool that will smooth the tape lines and make the heart wall perfect. You are made perfect in your surrender to His love.

When your walls are up, resting on a strong foundation, you are now ready for that movable barrier, a portal which allows entering and exiting, otherwise known as a door.

OPENING THE DOOR

Doors offer a form of protection. Windows are more functional, allowing natural light, ventilation, and views. When building a house on the foundation of God, you are given the keys to the door that no person can shut. In fact, in the Bible, God's prophet, Isaiah says, *"I will give him the key to the house of David—the highest position in the royal court. When he opens doors, no one will be able to close them; when he closes doors, no one will be able to open them"* (NLT Isaiah 22:22).

There is a cliché statement that when one door closes another door opens. I, too, have stood in the dark hallway while waiting for a new door to open. I don't know about you, but at night, those dark hallways feel creepy. They can be a little scary, especially when there are many doors and it's dark, quiet, and all you can hear is your breathing get more and more erratic. I have found over time that when God closes a door, he does not always announce, "Courtney, I have opened a new door for you, it is right here!" There have been times when I have had to feel my way down the pitch black hallway to find the open door. Alexander Graham Bell once said this, *"When one door closes, another opens; but we often look so long and regretfully at the closed door that we do not see the one that has been opened for us. Defeat is nothing but education; it is the first step towards something better"* (1955).

Is this you? Has God opened the door for you but you're staring so hard at the opportunity or relationship lost that you don't see it? This is your sign,— look up! Perhaps the window just needed to be opened. *"The eye is the lamp of the body; so if your eye is clear [spiritually perceptive], your whole body will be full of light [benefiting from God's precepts]. But if your eye is bad [spiritually blind], your whole body will be full of darkness [devoid of God's precepts]. So if the [very] light inside you [your inner self, your heart, your conscience] is darkness, how great and terrible is that darkness!"* (AMP Matthew 6:22-24) What are you watching, reading, viewing that impacts your inner home? Is it impacting you positively or negatively? This may be the sign you have been asking for. Take time to reflect on relationships and opportunities that seem to have stalled or come to an end.

THE FINISHING TOUCHES

As the remodeling comes to a close, you can begin to envision decorating the new space. Imagine how you will begin to use and enjoy this new space. This is where the joy of the Lord will live. This is the stage of life where celebration will take place. You have come through the dirt, dust, and muck of rebuilding the foundation. You have built upon the strong tower of the Lord and are now ready to enjoy what you have worked so hard for. It was not an easy task. Building never is. You are courageous, strong, and steadfast. God will continue to sustain you in all your ways as you continue to dwell with him in your thoughts, acts, and heart.

It is time to let down the inner walls that hold you back. Let those walls down. Doubt and fear have no place here. Imagine the walls of your heart lowering slowly, inch by inch, allowing the love of God to enter. I want you to picture your heart surrounded by four walls. Now, imagine that first wall slowly lowering. It is allowing the presence of God in. The warmth of his love slowly starts to creep up into your heart. Now take a deep breath. It is time to lower the second wall. As this wall lowers God's grace, his unmerited and underserving favor, mingles with his love. It is beginning to swirl around your heart. Let's begin to lower the third wall. As you begin to allow it to lower, God's mercy, His kindness, forgiveness, and empathy begins to flow in and through your heart. In fact, it has begun to gently soak into your heart, like a sponge; you are absorbing God's love. As the fourth wall is lowered, the walls of pain, pride, and offense are no longer found. Instead, your heart is free, filled with God's love, grace, and mercy as it begins to flow and mingle within you. Be sure to share this love, grace, and mercy with those around you. It is a gift that keeps on giving.

This is no easy task of tearing down and rebuilding. It is labor intensive. It requires blood, sweat, and comes with a few tears. I am so proud of you for beginning to work on your inner self and tackle such a huge project. I would like to pray the following prayer with you:

Dear God,

I thank you today for the strongholds on my life that have brought me this far. Though I may not understand them, I thank you for them because they have brought me closer to you today. Forgive me, God, for any lack of forgiveness in my heart that has allowed offense to take over. I ask you to please help me identify who I need to forgive and to release myself from the burden of pain. I ask you to help me to identify the strongholds of negativity in my life. Remove them from me right now in the name of Jesus. I thank you, Lord, that as I surrender those strongholds to you, I am filled with peace and acceptance of who I am today. I am grateful for the new beginning you have given me. I am thankful for the new foundation in your son Jesus and the new building that has begun to take place in my heart. I ask you to strengthen my foundation, walls, roof, doorways, and windows. I ask you to protect each and every entry and exit point of my heart. No weapon formed against me will prosper. I declare my new dwelling place will bring peace and comfort to those who are hurting. Let your light shine through me today and every day from now on.

In Jesus' name I pray...

Amen

Exercise

Identify a stronghold you need to tear down and a foundation you can begin to build. List three ways you can tear down that stronghold. List three ways you can begin to build your new foundation.

_____

_____

_____

_____

_____

_____

_____

_____

_____

_____

_____

_____

_____

_____

_____

_____

_____

_____

_____

_____

_____

CHAPTER 6

LAUGHING UNTIL YOU CRY

"A time to weep and a time to laugh."

Ecclesiastes 3:4a

I am tragically known for laughing at the worst times. Many perceive that my laughter is a disregard for the seriousness of the situation, or a lack of empathy. In reality, I laugh when nervous, stressed, sad, sarcastic, happy, and even angry. In some of the worst moments of my life I found laughter to be the one thing that helps me gain perspective. I have learned that either God or I have a quirky sense of humor, especially when He is showing me that He cares, hears me, and is in control. Dr. Lee Berk, who conducted a study at Loma Linda University in Southern California, says that laughter actually begins to change your brain chemistry and lowers your stress levels. (Ringer, 2019)

Which made me wonder, what makes you laugh, my friend? Laughter has a way of connecting people; socially it draws us closer and releases feel-good neurotransmitters that boost our moods. Here's the thing, though. When we are in a season that has caused us to weep, we find it hard to believe that a season of great joy is ever going to come. Maybe you have not experienced great sorrow in your life just yet. If it is not relatable now, go ahead and bookmark this chapter. One day, it will be.

"Even in laughter the heart may ache, and rejoicing may end in grief" (Proverbs 14:13 NIV). Life continues to go on even though we grieve, laugh, or are somewhere in between. How do you conjure up laughter when the weeping has just finished? I am speaking to those who have suffered extreme sorrow, those of you who have experienced heartache that makes you weep for days, months, and years. You who have wondered how and when the pain will stop. Sweet friend, pay attention. Your season of laughter is upon you. It is coming. In fact, that pain you have felt cannot compare to the joy that is coming. Every single tear has been accounted for. You will be repaid sevenfold for every tear of pain. All because you are deeply loved by God.

TIMING YOUR LAUGHTER

As I wrote this, trying to explain what is so important about the season of weeping and laughing, mourning, and dancing, I came to a standstill. Writers block kicked in and I stared at my blank screen for a long time. I was challenged to figure out how important time is in this season. A laugh at the wrong time can be viewed as disrespectful and untrustworthy. A cry at the wrong time and people think you have gone crazy, may be bipolar, or definitely had too much to drink. However, the biblical concept of time is very different. In biblical concepts and terms, God has control over time, but not to be controlling or fatalistic. He transcends over time, creating cycles of days and seasons for eternal purposes, not earthly ones. Which means your season of weeping, laughing, mourning, and dancing all have eternal connections. It is my purpose to help you understand your current season and how it has eternal effects.

REALLY BAD TIMING

Several years ago, my sister was diagnosed with cancer. Since I was unemployed then, I thought this would be the perfect time to travel the five-thousand miles to help her during her treatments. My sister begged me not to come, out of an abundance of caution. Traveling upped my risk of getting sick and bringing germs to her compromised immune system. Months later, her health continued to decline, and the timing to visit went out the door. My husband and I were selling our home, preparing to move, and I had just started a new job. When one morning, I received the call no one wants to receive from their parent. On my nephew's 21st birthday, his mother, my sister, entered heaven's gates and left the world behind.

With tear-filled eyes, I bought my emergency plane ticket for that evening. I quickly made several calls to arrange for help with my children, my job, realtor, and my husband. All the while, I was a ball of emotions: sad, hurt, scared, and angry. I didn't get to say goodbye. I didn't get the chance to say I love you one more time. I was concerned for my dad, sisters, and their families. That evening, I boarded the plane. It was a beautiful 82 degrees at home. When I landed 15 hours later, it was 5 in the evening and 9 degrees outside. I had not seen snow in over 20 years. I marveled at the snowflakes as my family drove me to my sister's house.

The next day, after an emotional wake, I sat at her kitchen counter, staring at the dancing sunflower toy that sat on her kitchen island. I learned it was a souvenir from one of her many trips. As I reflected on our not-so-close relationship, I questioned God: did my sister love me? Growing up, as the baby half-sister, I adored and looked up to my big sisters whenever they were around. The grief in the not knowing where I stood in my sister's heart clouded my brain. Regret flooded my heart; I wish we had had more time together.

After another day of services, I boarded a series of flights for the 14-hour trek home where I cried most of the way. Please be kind to the stranger crying her eyes out on the plane. I was a hot mess. After two days of recovery at home, I found myself needing to run a few errands before work. Plagued by the same thoughts of "Did she love me," I was a distracted driver. While I drove myself to the store, I had it out with God. I had a fussy temper tantrum right in the presence of God.

I demanded an answer to my heart cry, "Did she love me?" As I approached an intersection, life went into slow motion. I happened to look in my rearview mirror at the car behind me. Through my rear windshield, into their windshield, I saw a dancing sunflower on the dashboard. And I knew in that exact moment that this was my confirmation that it was my time to quit crying and begin laughing. And I did. I laughed like a crazy person, who cries, all the way to the store. Peace flooded my car in that moment. I felt so thoroughly and completely loved; I never questioned her love again.

RECOGNIZING THE MESSAGE OF HOPE

Being able to see the sunflower dance on the dashboard was no coincidence. The joy, peace, and love that covered me in that moment was evidence of the Holy Spirit. Galatians 5:22 says, *"But the Holy Spirit produces this kind of fruit in our lives: love, joy, peace, patience, kindness, goodness, faithfulness"* (NLT). We can determine the arrival of hope based upon these fruits. When we weep with joy, we have witnessed the tangible proof of our faith coming to pass. Even in our mourning we can experience the fruit of the spirit and find hope in other's kindness and goodness.

Let's dig a little deeper, shall we? I am going to challenge you to identify why you weep and mourn. Is it out of grief, regret, shame, anger, or sadness? Understanding helps identify how to move forward. When a person cries from shame and regret, repentance for our actions happens. This is good for our soul. It allows us to release ourselves from the past. When repentance flows, our admittance to wrongdoing releases the grip the devil has on our past. It allows us to turn and create a new life: away from the pain and suffering, toward a future that includes choices that are wise the purposeful.

When you cry out in anger, who are you angry at? Sometimes I have been so angry, hot tears poured down my face. Injustice stirs up my anger and it is a quick trigger. I have had times where I had to sit and figure out who am I truly angry at. Sometimes it was myself. I wanted to point the finger at someone else, but in reality it was my own actions that caused a consequence that I was angry about. Other times, we are victims to things that are truly unfair and painful. Stuff we have no control over, so we become angry with God. I get it, and so does God. Sometimes bad things happen for which I can give no logical explanation. People die at seemingly the wrong time. People hurt us and we are victims to pain that is unthinkable. I am going to challenge you to embrace that suck for a moment. Package it all up, all of that righteous anger. Now picture yourself walking to the altar of God. Go ahead, he's sitting there loving you and he knows how to turn the tables around for you. As you walk up to him, drop the package of anger. Give it all to him and release yourself from it. You see, God says he loves you with an everlasting and unfailing love (Jeremiah 31:3). Your anger at being unfairly treated is no surprise to him. Now watch him take all that pain and anger, and turn it around for your good!

TURNING THE TABLES

Years ago I asked myself, what if I had to experience this crappy season in order to be able to tell someone in 10 years that they, too, will survive and thrive after a similar season. That what seems like a tragedy today is the cause of great celebration tomorrow? That the stress, anxiety, and pain will actually be the very force that propels you forward into a future full of peace, acceptance, love and joy? What if every single tear you cried is to help someone else find peace in their own walk of pain? Would the pain be worth the struggle? For some, the answer is no, and that is perfectly all right. For me, the answer was yes, because if that one tear I had to cry helps tug your shirt back as you lean over the cliff, it was all worth it. The pain experienced requires you to take yourself out of the equation.

This is exactly what Jesus did when he accepted his fate and offered himself as a sacrifice on the cross (Romans 5:8). He said you are worth every lashing. You are worth the crown of thorns being pushed onto his head. Every single drop of blood and sweat that was poured out on the cross was a price he was willing to pay. He innocently hung on the cross like a criminal because he knew your life was worth living ... no matter what season you are in. Your tears mingled with his on the cross that day. His willing sacrifice tells us that he knew our worth before we ever did ourselves. He did it for your freedom. He wants you to be free from all pain that causes you to weep at night. Jesus believed that the temporary pain of the moment was worth your reward.

> *"She is clothed in strength and dignity;*
> *she can laugh at the days to come"*
>
> Proverbs 31:25 NIV

Now, you may not feel as selfless as Jesus did that day when he prayed for you (John 17); girl, I get it. But what if your story of pain could bring someone else hope tomorrow? Jesus knew that the pain was temporary. The crying would only last for a season. He knew that joy would come in the morning. He had faith that his Abba, his papa, would turn the tables and that the weeping would turn to laughter. A loving parent wants to see his child laugh and not suffer. You will laugh again; you will find your way through the struggle of mind-numbing nothing to the thrill of laughing until you cry. The pain of your today will make the laughter and dancing of tomorrow that much sweeter. How else could we know how priceless the sound of laughter is without understanding what it means to be without it?

I never want to trivialize your time of crying or the pain attached to it. But if you allow yourself to welcome the stillness and ask Jesus to show up, I promise you, he will. How he does will be different for each of us. Because he knows your heart so well, he will show up in a special way, just for you. Let us pray for the laughter that brings tears.

Dear God,

I want to thank you for today. Thank you for the seasons of crying and the seasons of laughter. It is with awesome wonder I ask you to lend me your eyes, ears, and understanding of this season. I pray for those who have made me cry. Bless them, Father. Cover them with your love and heal their wounds. God, please help me to use my time in the season for good. Please come into my heart and be with me in my seasons of weeping and those of laughter. I ask you to please forgive me when I was less than kind to those who were suffering in their season. I ask you to please protect me as I seek you in my moments of joy and sorrow. Open my eyes so that I may see you in my darkest moments of crying and in my brightest moments of laughter. I thank you for showing yourself to me.

In Jesus' name I pray...

Amen

Exercise

Quiet yourself in your moment of crying or laughing and ask Jesus into the moment. Write that moment down and reflect on just how well he showed up for you.

_____

_____

_____

_____

_____

_____

_____

_____

_____

_____

_____

_____

_____

_____

_____

_____

_____

_____

_____

_____

_____

_____

CHAPTER 7

MOURNING INTO DANCING

"A time to mourn and a time to dance."

Ecclesiastes 3:4b

As you transition from laughing and crying, remember that the Bible shows us there is a time to mourn and a time to dance. At a first glance, those seasons were so similar they were the same... until I dug a little deeper. You see, to mourn means we feel or show deep sorrow or regret, usually at the loss of someone or something, often from them passing away. Different than simply weeping, mourning is a deeper experience. It is a season that brings intense change to one's life. Dancing implies a joyful nature. It is an expression of one's happiness and excitement for a season. Finding the hope in each of these seasons requires a fierce determination to stay focused on being resilient. Wayne Dyer once said, *"When you dance, your purpose is not to get to a certain place on the floor. It's to enjoy each step along the way."* (Dyer) Somehow, some way, you have to continue to reach for the hem of Jesus' garment.

MOURNING YOUR LOSS

I mourned the loss of a child for over 14 years. Each year the stabbing pain of heartache would send me to my bed for the day. I would relive the season over and over, wondering and believing I could have done something to alter the course of action. I did not know how to find hope in the loss of my child, and no one shared with me or taught me how to grieve that loss. I had to teach myself how to be released from the burden of pain and embrace gratitude for the life and children I do have. I believed that if I let go from the pain of the past, I would be letting go of the possibility of hope that was lost so long before. I learned that in surrendering to what was, I found peace and love in moving out of the season of mourning. In that peace and love, I realized that this is what every parent wants for their child and what every child wants from their parent: to live a life of joy and gladness in spite of pain and sorrow.

Twenty years after experiencing my own devastating loss I found myself working in a funeral home. Of all the places I thought I would work, this was not one of them. However, it was an honor to sit with members of my community while helping them plan a service in one of their darkest moments in life. I learned many lessons that year. The wisdom that many bestowed upon me was significant. The insight that was shared over and over was this, your loved one, who passed on would not want you to suffer. I have sat with countless families who were in shock at the passing of their beloveds. While I listened to their stories of bravery, humor, charitable deeds, love, and wit, they all had one thing in common: Not one of them ever said their loved one would want them to be broke, suffer, or be sad at their passing. Every person I spoke with said that the person who had just passed away would want them to be happy, fulfilled, full of life, and to live a life of abundance. Not one of them was perfect. They came from different demographics, religious affinity, race, creed, sexual identity, and income levels. Some had dementia before they passed, and their loved ones spoke highly of who they were before they became sick. Some passed away in tragic circumstances: suicides, car accidents, and murders. Some were addicted to substances they could not quit. For every person I sat with, their grief and shock was tangible. I sat and mourned with them. Each one had a story that our meeting was too short to cover completely. A common thread among them all was that the one who had passed would not want the ones who remain to suffer, be angry, sad, or stay in grief for too long. They would want those left on earth to live with joy and love.

The lessons learned in watching others grieve were many. Some sound cheesy and cliche; life is short, count your blessings. The hardest one to embrace was this: we all have to pass away at some time. We have to come to grips that those around us will die too. Either we will be at their funerals or they will be at ours. Only God knows when that will be. This knowledge has made me picky about what I would mourn in the future. There will be times of recognition, such as calling that person is not possible. Hanging out is not an option. And without a doubt, these moments cause tears of sadness, anger or even bitterness, because calling that loved one on a hard day would be a comfort. This is when God will send you what you need for companionship, love, encouragement, and support. I have seen time and time again how He moves people into position at just the right time, connecting them to those they can love, encourage, and support too.

The processes of grief and mourning are complex. It is natural to do one of two things: either sit in isolation and do nothing, or go out in public and distract yourself. Sometimes you flip-flop between both. There will be times when sitting is what you need to do, and other times, you need to jump up and get some fresh air and feel alive again. There is a season to reflect and process your emotions. It is the transition between mourning and dancing. This is where you begin to see glimmers of hope shine through. Years ago, my friend lost two family members back to back. She was shaken and confused when she reached out to me for support. She asked if there was a time frame on grieving for the loss of her family members. In short, the answer is no. There is no way to say you have to do x, y, and z to heal. Yes, there are healthy and unhealthy coping mechanisms for grief. I do not suggest you drink yourself under the table every day. I pray you find a healthy outlet for your grief. Walks help. Walks with supportive friends help more. Finding a hobby helps too. And when you find a hobby, let me know. Apparently, I do not have any and I am in dire need of finding one!

> *"So with you: Now is your time of grief;*
> *but I will see you again and you will rejoice,*
> *and no one will take away your joy."*
>
> John 16:22 NIV

DANCING FOR DAYS

Have you become fed up with mourning? At some point you will reach a transition point and begin to crave change. How quickly that happens is not important to your healing. It's only important that it does happen. Whether it is through social interaction, public events, or even a trip to the store, your time of mourning will come to a close and your time of dancing will begin. Martha Graham once said, *"Dance is the hidden language of the soul of the body. And it's partly the language that we don't want to show"* (1985) Dancing in praise and worship is mentioned in the Bible several times, usually in reference to gladness and joy: a movement that celebrates of overcoming defeat. Jeremiah 31:13 says, *"I will turn their mourning into gladness; I will give them comfort and joy instead of sorrow."*

With gladness, we have gratitude. Being thankful for what has occurred changes perspectives and outlooks on situations. Say you're upset about being passed over for a promotion. Perhaps the one who passed you over is a trusted individual or friend. I get it. Here's the thing, though: You can sit and be upset for 5 minutes or a day or a week. It will not change the outcome. You can choose to allow yourself to feel the disappointment, shame, regret. Allow each emotion to flow through you, but don't allow it to stay. Release it and find a way to be grateful that is the present moment is good. One of the hardest scriptures to relate to is 1 Thessalonians 5:18 (The Passion Translation): *"And in the midst of everything be always giving thanks, for this is God's perfect plan for you in Christ Jesus."* Giving thanks during periods of mourning is acknowledging God in your time of greatest distress and recognizing that He is sovereign over our world and you trust in His sovereignty to bring you comfort and peace in your hardest moment.

You can choose to be graceful in your season of mourning. It brings the season of dancing closer, faster. You have witnesses by your side, watching how you handle this season of mourning and pain. Your response to rejection and redirection says a lot more about you than a promotion. John Rohn says this, *"You must take personal responsibility. You cannot change the circumstances, the seasons, or the wind; but you can change yourself. That is something you have charge of."* (investigate.com, 2017) You can mourn and dance within days of each other, or you can mourn and dance years apart. Dancing for the Lord implies faith in God, either for what he has done, or in what he will do for you.

DEPLETING DOUBT

God knows you may be grieving and yet still choose to offer up a sacrifice of praise. It is a sweet sound to His ears because he knows the grief causes you to stumble. It blinds you. Being real with God pleases him. Shouting, telling him you're angry, declaring, "It's not fair." He knows. And He knows in your willingness to praise when you want to mourn, healing begins. The raw cutting edge of your heart begins to soften and heal. As you begin to let your inner guard down, let the grief flow, He turns the grief to gladness.

God will turn your wailing into dancing. Psalm 30:11-12 says, *"You turned my wailing into dancing; you removed my sackcloth and clothed me with joy, that my heart may sing your praises and not be silent. Lord my God, I will praise you forever."* It is not time to pretend that you are happy. Sister, this is about activating hope deep within you. It's about taking the mourning and stirring up your spirit, taking the breath God gave you this morning and using it to thank him. The Holy Spirit will descend upon you. As you begin to look at this season and understand that it is changing, you will notice a change in your heart as well.

Festivals marked the change of seasons. At the festival, there is always an abundance of food, lights, and music. The festivals are to celebrate the harvest that had come forth after months or years of preparation and waiting. Sometimes farmers have to deal with loss, and they mourn for their losses too. But, always, at the festival, there was dancing. Dancing to celebrate the harvest, to fellowship and enjoy each other's company. Joy abounds on the dance floor!

My sweet friend, the seasons and cycles of mourning and dancing cannot be avoided. They can, however, be embraced. The darkness of mourning is lessened with the promise of a new day. Offer gratitude for the process even when you don't understand it. God knows how hard that sacrifice of praise is; it is what makes it so precious and holy. I want to pray for you as you journey from mourning to dancing or dancing to mourning, say this prayer with me today, sweet friend.

Dear God,

Your mercies are new every morning. Let me hear in the morning of your steadfast love, for in you I trust. Make me know the way I should go, for to you I lift up my soul. You have been with me in the fire of mourning as I journey into the season of dancing. I thank you for being by my side every step of the way. Thank you for dancing with me, holding me as we spin and laugh. I thank you for holding my shoulders as I mourn the loss of time, money, relationships, partners, children, homes, jobs, and myself. Take my pain, Father. In exchange, I receive your love, hope, grace, and mercy. Take my ashes and make me beautiful. I surrender my heart and life to you, Lord. Take all of me as I journey through this season. I love you, Lord, for never leaving my side. Even when I see no way, you are my way-maker. Dance with me, Abba, as we celebrate the season of harvests yet to come. I will celebrate you with every breath I take. For all that I am angry about in my loss, I pray for peace to overflow my heart, home, work, and relationships. I pray for restoration of my family, life, and soul. Open my eyes to your presence in this season. Open my ears to hear your whisper as I go about my day.

In Jesus' name I pray...

Amen

Exercise

Identify three areas of your life on which to focus in prayer. Write those areas in the space below.

_____

_____

_____

_____

_____

_____

_____

_____

_____

CHAPTER 8

DISTRIBUTING GOODNESS

"A time to scatter stones and a time to gather them."

Ecclesiastes 3:5a

The real question is, who the heck needs stones in their life besides for landscaping or to build a cozy fireplace? In what way, shape, or form does the scattering of stones or gathering of stones apply to me? I am a modern-day woman who lives in suburbia and drives a minivan, for crying out loud. But digging down into the depths of biblical history and discovering the significance of stones created a life-changing "aha!" moment for me. Stones were used for a variety of reasons. Stones, boulders and rocks served as landmarks, altars and weapons. Gemstones were used as gifts, adornment and a commodity. It is time to examine the various ways stones can be relatable to modern day living.

ALTERING REALITY

Breaking up can be good. Breaking up cookies to make a pie crust is good. Breaking up a fight between siblings is a daily occurrence and also good.

However, upon first glance at "a time to scatter stones and a time to gather them" (Ecclesiastes 3:5) I became confused and did not understand how this season applied to my life. Breaking up stones, had me staring at the page with a giant "HUH?" over my head. What is the message here? "A time to scatter stones and a time to gather them" really does not apply to my daily life. I am no farmer, and certainly not a landscaper. In Hawaii we have lava rocks. They are black, porous, and sharp! And these are the rocks that came to my mind when I read this scripture. What importance does lava rock have in my life? In Hawaii, we often use lava rock to build walls, fences, and even water features. But I am not doing that, so to me, rocks are useless. Moreover, why would I want to scatter them? They hurt to step on barefoot! The scattering stones I could think of are those little bits of gray gravel used in yard and construction projects. You know the ones that get stuck in your shoes when you walk through them? The ones 2-year-old boys love to pick up and throw. Those scatter like crazy. Scattering something larger than gravel-sized rocks would be tiresome. Heavy and inconvenient, large stones would be almost impossible to scatter. Or would they?

As we dive into the importance of gathering stones and scattering them, you will find that this process can be applied practically and powerfully to your life. In the Bible, the scattering of stones meant the removal of stones from a building, wall, or farming site. The action of gathering stones was for collecting building materials for a project; in this biblical context, it was specifically for laying a foundation of a structure of some kind. Stones were used for altars, boundary lines, and landmarks, even as weapons. Each season will require us to gather stones for various ourposes. Sometimes we gather to build, while at others we must scatter stones because they serve no purpose or value for us.

If you can learn how to identify the purpose of your stones, then you will begin to usher in clarity and hope for the situation. The altars, walls, and landmarks you created in your heart and mind served a purpose in your life. But at some point you must recognize they are no longer serving you. Perhaps your boundary lines have shifted and you have increased your territory: you had a new child or you have new love to give. You got a promotion and now have more responsibility at work. You bought a new home with a larger piece of land. Perhaps, you fell in love and now have two lives have joined together instead of one. All of these are reasons to shift your boundary line. You will need to move or scatter your stones to do that.

Perhaps the altar you built is no longer serving you. The sacrifices you have been making may not be working in your life. Now is the time to evaluate that altar and discern whether it is truly helping you live the life you want to create for yourself. Is that job really getting you where you want to be? Is that relationship dull or does it cause you to improve yourself?

Are you perhaps worshiping the wrong god? The altar is a place where we put our offerings, sacrifices, in an expression of worship and thanksgiving. Let me ask you this, who and what are you worshipping that is no longer serving you or God?

Breaking down the old that is not serving you makes room for something that will be useful and of greater value. Is it worth scattering the stones and dismantling the altar? Let me ask you, is your mental, physical, financial and eternal health worth it? Is the end result worth the monumental effort needed to tear down the walls that keep you from being whole? Or do you just leave it as it is, broken, in disrepair? Does it look like that house on the street that everyone avoids because it's a mess, a shanty, run- down and scary-looking. Is it better to tear it down, remove the mess, and start with a clean slate?

PLACING LANDMARKS

All of your land, all of you, needs to have boundary markers to claim your territory. It is marked for a special purpose, owned and managed by a certain individual. These boundaries are necessary to identify the land and its purpose. In times of travel, landmarks were critical in identifying locations of provision, shelter, and protection. Just like land, our hearts have boundaries too. We only let certain people in, while others we allow to approach the gate, but not onto the land. And then there are those who get zero access whatsoever.

What landmarks do you have set up that mark the territory of your heart? Are there any that can be moved due to a healing that has taken place? Perhaps it is time to allow your loved one back in. They have paid the price, they have changed and they too, deserve grace. Or are you ready to put some landmarks up? Are you ready to tell someone they are not allowed to trespass on your territory? That's great too!

GATHERING UP GOODNESS

When you have a gotten rid of restraining relationships, jobs, hobbies, or habits, you have loosed yourself from commitments that no longer serve you. You are now ready to build! You are ready to gather up good stones for purposes that have generational gains. Seasons of hardship will no longer cause you to fear, but instead will bring excitement because you know good is coming afterward. The stone altar, the landmark you place will be to memorialize the miracle that occurred in that season. *"Ancient altars were raised structures that people placed sacrifices on, almost exclusively built as a monument to remember or commemorate a divine occurrence which took place at a certain location."* (bible-history.com).

As you gather your stones, I want you to picture what that looks like. Are they smooth stones you use for massages? Are they pet-rock sized? Or are they boulders of different sizes? Different stones have different purposes. An altar in biblical times was often a single piece of uncut stone, similar to a table, upon which an item to be sacrificed was laid. Today, we no longer use stone altars in churches, fields, or at our homes. To many, those altars are now only in our hearts; they are metaphorical places in our minds. If you attend church, the front of it may be considered an altar. Here, there is often a table or podium of sorts. This is where some churches call the people forward if they want to receive a prayer or to sing and dance in worship. However, for this book, I am referring to the altars in our hearts and minds; those places we have erected emotionally as markers of past hurts or celebrations.

Thousands of years ago, stone altars served as places of worship and as places to remember a covenant, originally God's covenant with His people. It memorialized his promise of protection, provision, and love. Altars were traditionally placed at the location of the divine occurrence. In Genesis 28:10-19, Jacob had a dream in which God promised that the land he was sleeping on would be the land of his descendants for generations to come. Jacob had used a stone as a pillow (I know, I know, who does that?), and when he woke up, he took that stone pillow, poured oil on it in as an act of anointing, and then erected it in that spot to mark the place as a holy, as promised by God. He even began to refer to that place by a different name. The city had a new identity (Genesis 28:19) due to a covenant promise from God; the stone memorialized the promise and relationship to Jacob and his descendants.

It was a big deal, it was a big promise, one that required faithfulness in order to keep. He had to grasp onto hope even when situations seemed hopeless. He could not place jobs, materialism, people, or ambition before God. This would have created false idols, false altars that detracted away from God and His promise. It meant Jacob had to acknowledge that God was his provider. Any marker, indicator, stone, etc., that takes away from the markers of God must scattered to find hope and peace. The landmarks that put God second, third, fourth, last? Those need to be scattered and rearranged to allow for God's to be first.

FLINGING STONES

Do you know the story of David and Goliath? The story of the young man who volunteered to fight the giant to win a war? It took great courage and faith to overcome the seemingly impossible task of fighting an infamous warrior. In hand–to-hand combat, David did not stand a chance of winning. However, the stones David carried proved to be a weapon with more than enough power to knock someone out from a distance, meaning he did not even have to get dirty! Girl, do you know how amazing this is? God provided EXACTLY what David needed to do the impossible … with stones! The stones referenced in the Bible were no pebble-sized pieces of gravel. Oh, no, they were roughly the size of tennis balls. They were handcrafted and adored just as highly as any finely crafted sword.

Am I a finely honed, unique stone, created for a special purpose? Perhaps God wants to put me in the slingshot to defeat the giant you are facing. Sister, you too are a stone in the slingshot about to be unleashed, for the purpose of defeating the enemy. Girl, you have power! What giant is standing in front of you, calling you out? Saying you cannot accomplish that which you have set out to do? The giant that is taunting you with words of accusation, disapproval, judgment, and blame? Defending yourself with your own words, in your own strength, may work for a while, but it does not have eternal effects. The weapon you have at your disposal, your stone to your personal Goliath, is the word of God. You are not fighting in the physical world; you are fighting in the spiritual. Your stone is perfect. There is no way it can fail with scripture. Even Jesus used it when the devil tried to taunt him (Matthew 4:4). 2 Corinthians 10:3-5 says, *"For though we live in the world, we do not wage war as the world does. The weapons we fight with are not the weapons of the world. On the contrary, they have divine power to demolish strongholds. We demolish arguments and every pretension that sets itself up against the knowledge of God, and we take captive every thought and make it obedient to Christ."*

MILLING STONES

I don't know about you, but for me the weight of negativity, doubt, despair, hopelessness, fear, and anger are heavy. They drain us of energy that could be put to better use. It eventually weights a person down to the point that getting out of bed is hard. It clouds judgment and results in faulty decision-making. Sometimes the mundane and simple things in life are too heavy to sift through. They are as heavy as a millstone used back in the day to grind wheat into flour. These burdens are just too much. This is when scattering stones is so important to your prosperity. We can lighten our load. Jesus reassures us that he is able to carry your heavy burden. Jesus calls to every person, regardless of creed, religion, nationality, race, or sexual orientation. He says to you and every single person you know and love, in Matthew 11:28-30 (MSG), *"Are you tired? Worn out? Burned out on religion? Come to me. Get away with me and you'll recover your life. I'll show you how to take a real rest. Walk with me and work with me—watch how I do it. Learn the unforced rhythms of grace. I won't lay anything heavy or ill-fitting on you. Keep company with me and you'll learn to live freely and lightly."*

If you are in a place of wondering, questioning where God is in this moment, I encourage you to ask him to reveal himself to you. Jesus promises that if we "ask, it will be given to you; seek, and you will find; knock, and it will be opened to you" (Matthew 7:7). As you make a new boundary for your life, make sure that your heart reflects the value of the land within it. Sister, your heart is valuable. Your story has worth. The impact you have to make on the world matters!

You are strong and beautiful. You are fearfully and wonderfully made (Psalm 139:14).

PRECIOUS STONES

Last, but not least, there are precious stones. Did you know that wisdom is considered a precious stone? In Proverbs 3:13-15, wisdom is more precious than jewels and nothing that can be desired is as precious as wisdom. Leonardo da Vinci once said that, *"Wisdom is the daughter of experience."* I know you are wise, dear sister. You have experienced life that has caused you to rise up in wisdom in order to survive. You have pearls of wisdom to share with other sisters who need to hear you. What measure of hope can you share with someone who feels defeated? When you generously share your words of wisdom, God will supply you with even more. Never hoard your precious stones for yourself. God is waiting to hand you more as you hand out what is in you. Give yours away with grace and truth. Share with a patient love for those who are desperate for a peek of more.

SETTING THE STONE

So sis, here you are, armed with stones for warfare, on ground anointed with landmarks and altars. You are dressed in precious stones and ready to battle the Goliath in front of you. What are you going to do with the stones you have been given? Are you ready to share with the world that which has been given to you? Are you ready to lay down your fears and pick up the stones of wisdom to conquer new territory? It is time set up your landmark to protect the land which has been gifted to you. Generations of family members are waiting for you to ask, seek, and knock for answers from God. Before we move on, let's pray for wisdom:

Dear God,

You are so amazing. I pray, Father God, for your stones. I ask you, Father, to help me identify altars that are unpleasant to you. Lend me the strength and wisdom to tear them down. I seek you presence in my life as I erect new landmarks that set me apart as your child. My burden has been heavy and I am tired from laboring for so long. Please come into my heart and take my yoke. I receive your yoke in exchange. In fact, I already feel the burden lifting. Thank you for your gentleness; your kindness soothes my soul. As I knock on your door today, I pray you awaken all of my senses to your presence. Help me to scatter the stones of generosity, grace, wisdom, and love to those who are in desperate need. I trust you to provide for my needs continually as I seek your will in all that I do. Please protect my land, Father God. I declare Psalm 91 and a hedge of protection around me, my family, my job, and those I love. I thank you again for all that you are.

In Jesus' name I pray...

Amen

Exercise

What new identity do you want?

Identify one altar or landmark that causes confusion or chaos. List three ways you know it is in the wrong place in your life.

What is the giant taunting you with? What inner dialogue do you hear repeatedly in your mind?

What kind of precious stone do you consider wisdom to be? Picture that stone around your neck at all times. Keep it close to your heart.

_____

_____

_____

_____

_____

_____

_____

CHAPTER 9

DECIDING WHAT YOU EMBRACE

"A time to embrace and a time to refrain from embracing."

Ecclesiastes 3:5b

Embracing rejection hurts like a mother, doesn't it? Did you know that Oprah Winfrey was publicly fired from her first television job as an anchor in Baltimore for getting "too emotionally invested" in her stories? Her season of rejection turned into a season of rejoicing when she embraced who she was and became bigger and more successful than all of those who did not embrace her. Those who have not embraced you were not meant to come with you into your next season of life. They have to remain apart, and not move with you into your future. Embracing the suck is never easy; however, when we do so with grace, the spiritual transformation that takes place is worth the price. A butterfly has to go through being a caterpillar and then remained wrapped under pressure in its cocoon before it can fly.

GRASPING ONTO LIFE

Embrace in Hebrew means to fasten on, as armor, to clasp in the arms with affection, to take in the arms; to hug, to cherish to love. An embrace is intimate and allows for closeness that requires a level of trust. I swear there is such a thing as a hug ministry. There are people gifted with the ability and know how to give the best hugs just when you need them. Did you know that a 20-second hug is powerful enough to relieve stress and pain? One 20-second hug can reduce inflammation, improve wound healing, and even lessen cravings for drugs, alcohol, and sweets. In that case, I'm about 25 hugs from 5 pounds of weight loss.

Here's the thing: To fully appreciate these hugs, you have to be willing to allow for the intimacy—the closeness—of such an experience. In keeping it real, many of us have been hurt physically, mentally, spiritually, and emotionally, which has kept our desire for intimacy in check. Maybe that describes you, and trusting others is not something you find easy. I get it. I've been there too. I am so sorry you had to experience that level of pain. Hugging someone when you are not ready to be vulnerable is just as nerve-wracking as the stress itself. If we can allow just one or two people in, however, it helps. Can I share with you what have learned in the process of growing in the season of embrace and refraining from embracing?

The trust factor is a key component. We are living in uncertain times, where we question who and what is trustworthy and what is not. Is it not the same with our relationship with God? I want to trust and receive an encouraging embrace from God, but it would also mean I have to trust Him to not hurt me in the process. God, being so good, knows that we might distrust Him. And so he sent us a word of promise of the good that comes from trusting in him. It is found in Proverbs 3:5-6 in The Passion Translation (TPT), which says, *"Trust in the Lord completely, and do not rely on your own opinions. With all your heart rely on Him to guide you, and He will lead you in every decision you make. Become intimate with Him in whatever you do, and He will lead you wherever you go."* Sister, when you do this, when you accept the embrace of the love of God, freedom is at hand. This freedom allows you to embrace new possibilities, relationships, careers, homes, and lives.

WELCOMING RESISTANCE

"Embrace the glorious mess that you are" (Murphy & Gilbert, 2011). Listen, your mess that you created is not a surprise to God. In fact, if you embrace the moment and trust Him, he can turn it into a beautiful message of hope. In fact, there is someone sitting at their own kitchen table wondering how they are going to get out of the exact same mess you are coming out of. You are qualified by God and that is more than enough.

In certain moments of my life, I have resisted the time to be still. In fact, I hate being still. Yet it has been those still seasons of life in which I have experienced the greatest moments of spiritual, mental, and emotional growth. I thrive on what I thought was being "helpful" and "busy" because I was taught that if you sit around and do nothing, you are lazy. Thanks to this mindset, I have put myself into seasons of chaos! I embraced the chaos because I thought that it meant that I was successful. I wasn't being lazy after all. I was busy, busy, busy! Until. I. Crashed. I had placed myself into positions of being needed, which were probably more enabling than helpful. I undervalued my personal time and energy, and certain aspects of my life began to unravel. It was in a split second that I was forced to take a time out. I took time off from work. I went back to ground zero. I was forced to sit and embrace the quiet alone time with myself, God, and my family. I had to learn to appreciate it as a gift rather than a curse. And honestly, that took some time. In that season, God revealed to me just how precious he considers his daughters. How often he showed up when I least expected him to. He told me that I no longer needed to be busy or do something for someone else to have worth. I no longer had to please others to be seen as valuable. I was enough for simply being me: broken, fragile, hysterical, angry, sad, and sometimes, unappreciative.

Maybe you're one of those confident girls who had worth and value taught to you as a little girl, and you embraced it. You never questioned it. Great. I am so eternally glad that this concept does not apply to you.

But there are too many sisters who doubt their worth and value. For you, my sweet friend, I encourage you to EMBRACE Jesus and welcome him into your heart and mind right now. He will meet you where you are at. It does not matter what you have done, who you slept with, or what drugs you have done.

In those moments when I felt the most unlovable, God showed up and embraced me. And because he is so amazing and good, he will show up and embrace you too. This is your moment to recognize you are standing at the door to a new season of profound growth and change. Change can cause our minds to resist anything and everything related to revolution. Ali Vincent once said, *"Resistance is never the agent of change. You have to embrace the actions that are going to get you closer to your goal."* (Vincent, 2009)

Are you in a season of resistance, of avoiding drawing close to others? Have you found that those in your clique, sphere of influence, or family no longer relate to you because you have passed up time with them? Was it for a season of growth? Or was it for a season of being stagnant? While you are in your season of refraining from gathering, embracing, loving on others, understand this: this too shall pass. Make sure that your time is being well-spent on building relationships with those who are in alignment with your values, beliefs, and goals. I love this quote by Hans F. Hansen, which says, *"People inspire you, or they drain you—pick them wisely."* (Hansen) The time to refrain from embracing is just as important as the time to embrace. Each has its turn in our lives to grow, love, heal, and help ourselves and others.

DECLINING THE DRAMA

It is time to decline the relationships, hobbies, and mindsets that drain you of energy. Your season of draining, toxic behaviors and relationships is no longer helping you get to where you really want to be in life. Curb your pride and do not allow yourself to be swooped up into an embrace from the devil. Girl, you can love many from afar, and trust God to step into their place in your life. I am praying for you as you read this: I pray God sends you relationships, connections, jobs, and opportunities that align with your calling. That He sends a restoration of fractured and broken relationships as you walk away from toxic ties. Yes, Lord, cover your daughters in love. Release them from embraces that have hurt them. Open their eyes to strategic moments of opportunity that bring them freedom. Amen. It is in that moment I see you, my sister, finding the bold strength to embrace this new season with fierce determination. I see opportunities that bring peace and not confusion. You display boldness that fascinates you and your loved ones. A gentleness that attracts those who are broken. I see grace that speaks of the miracles God is continuously pouring out over you. People will see your transformation. Rest assured, God already sees you and loves you just the way you are.

Let's pray for the season of embracing and refraining from it.

Dear God,

Welcome into this space. I embrace you into my heart right now. I accept your loving kindness as I transition through this season of my life. I thank you for creating me to be here in this moment with you. I do not understand why this season has had to happen. I do not know how you are going to show up and I am afraid. Being vulnerable is hard for me and I know you know why. Heal me, Lord, so that I am free to embrace all that you have for me in my life. Give me the strength and wisdom to know when to refrain from embracing opportunities, relationships, and thoughts that are not of you. Help me to pass up on the drama, and embrace the life of security with you. I love you, Lord, and look forward to feeling your embrace in my sleep this evening.

In Jesus' name I pray...

Amen

Exercise _____

This season of embracing and avoiding embrace looks different to each of us. What does it look like to you?

What steps are you ready to take to embrace peace, growth, love, and humility into your life today?

What are you willing to refrain from embracing in order to heal, love, and grow as God's child?

List three ways you can politely say no to situations that are no longer comfortable and cause you to avoid healing.

_____

_____

_____

_____

_____

_____

CHAPTER 10

SEARCHING FOR ANSWERS

"A time to search and a time to give up"

Ecclesiastes 3:6a

What are you searching for? Henry David Thoreau said, "Not until we are lost do we begin to find ourselves." (Thoreau) As women, many of us get caught up in the day–to-day life of juggling schedules, families, social lives, work, and hobbies. We slowly lose ourselves until one day we are staring at our reflection, wondering who the woman in the mirror is. We seem older, but the little girl inside is begging to come out. The core of who we are has been lost while running around living this thing we call life. Or maybe you have not had a chance to learn who you are. You have not had the freedom to be vulnerable with yourself, much less with someone else. Always having to be the strong one, pulling it together to make it all work out. Maybe the addiction, alcohol, or abuse was overwhelming and covered up who you are. Being bullied has caused you to hide your true self so deep inside that no one can find you, not even yourself.

Embracing a future of freedom will cause you to search for answers to the questions of your heart. What happens if the answer you seek can't be found? What, and how, will you move forward with hope? It starts with understanding what you are seeking and how willing you are to surrender and give up when the time is right.

SEARCHING FOR WHAT?

Someone once told me, be careful when you begin to search for answers; you may not be able to handle what you find. I thought this was a profound statement, given that so many search for hope. In fact, when I Googled this statement, there were 574,000,000 results at the time of this writing. How is it possible that there are millions of results, yet so many struggle to find it when they are searching? Let's start with three things we can search for in God:

1. **Strength** – Isaiah 40:28-29
2. **Provision** – Psalm 22:26
3. **Direction** – Proverbs 3:6

STRENGTH

"I'm too weak. I do not have the mental strength to handle this." Have you ever felt you have no ability to carry on? You were so weakened by life that silently you cried out for strength? And yet here you are, surviving 100% of the worst days ever. It seems as though you received strength, didn't you? I love Isaiah 40:28-29, as it reassures us that God is listening even when we do not speak aloud, and he answers us by empowering up to move with increasing strength. In this scripture the prophet Isaiah is letting the people of Israel know that God is so amazing, and he has enough strength to carry the world and everyone in it. In the TPT he declares, "Don't you know? Haven't you been listening? Yahweh is the one and only everlasting God, the Creator of all you can see and imagine! He never gets weary or worn out. His intelligence is unlimited; he is never puzzled over what to do! He empowers the feeble and infuses the powerless with increasing strength." Girl, he infuses us with his strength! How awesome is that! He does not simply pour out onto you; God makes it permeate throughout your body and spirit to a point that it will now ooze out of you. It is like a bubbling water fountain that never stops. It is for the purpose of helping someone else who needs to be encouraged and strengthened too. This is the tangible result of hope found in strength.

PROVISION

As he clearly provides strength, he provides when we are in need. And this is a hard one, sis. Because I just know some of you are wondering, where was he when I needed out? And I am telling you, I too have wondered where my out was. My rent, medicine, healing, rescue, car, care, or even love? And you know what, sis, when I look back at those situations, if I had had what I thought I needed in that moment, I would not have learned how to overcome, how to problem solve, how to work hard, and at times, how to do without. It builds character, strength, and faith. Is it easy? HELL NO. However, I have always had my basic needs met. There was a time that I once went without money for food and was too prideful to ask for assistance. I kept saying, "God will provide!" Well sisters, lesson learned; God provides in many ways.

You know what happened? My husband pestered me for days to apply for certain governmental assistance that I thought we did not want to receive or need. Finally, after a few days of staring at empty bank accounts, worry crept in ... OK, OK, truthfully, panic overwhelmed me. And then, only then, did I decide to pray, "God, if You want me to apply for this, can You please provide a parking stall right in front so I do not have to search for a stall? This way I know it is You confirming this is the right thing for me to do." Oh boy, testing the holiest of holies, I know. Did I mention how stubborn and bratty I can be? Can you imagine, God on his throne, looking down at me issuing ultimatums? Oh LAWD! Forgive. Me. Well, that day I went down to the location, and I kid you not, right in front of the door was an open metered parking stall. As I got out I scrambled to find a quarter for the meter and could not find one. So I turn to look at the meter and WHAT!? There are 19 minutes left on the clock. It was enough time for me to run inside, pull a number, receive an application and come back to my car, with 1 minute left. Back in my car, I cried big, fat crocodile tears of repentance, love, and gratitude. He provided for all of my needs in that moment and answered my bratty demand for reassurance. You see, God is not simply going to provide and then leave you high and dry without direction for where you are to go with that provision. Provision actually serves a second purpose in our season as it always includes direction.

DIRECTION

A distracted driver can easily go off course and lose direction. The navigation unit has to recalculate and prompt you to redirect your course as you travel to your destination. Ugh ... that process and that voice can be annoying, can't it? And then it constantly prompts you to "safely make a U-turn" in the most frustrating way as you navigate semi-trucks, three lanes of traffic, crying kids, and the radio, which you have to turn down in order to see better. We get off course and somehow have to get back on track, with God's direction navigating us through our spiritual traffic. Try to turn down God's voice and the results involve circling the same block over and over again until we get our sense of direction in order.

Proverbs 3:6 in the Voice Translation says, *"Give him credit for everything you accomplish, and He will smooth out and straighten the road that lies ahead."* Another translation says, *"Become intimate with Him in whatever you do, and he will lead you wherever you go"* (TPT). But my favorite translation says, "In all your ways know and acknowledge and recognize Him and He will make your paths straight and smooth [removing obstacles that block your way]." As you continue to seek God's direction for your path, He will drop personalized hints and clues that let you know you are on the right path. You will flow as you move. Even when you hit a speed bump or something else slows you down, he will supernaturally make a way as you continually seek him to navigate the roads. You will begin to cruise in your season.

In this season of seeking, God with all of His strength, provision, and direction will be more than enough to help you give up your pride, prejudices, and plays for control.

GIVING UP IS HARD

The Hebrew definition of give up is to yield, as in to give forth, send up, hand over, or to yield fruit. Remember at the beginning of this book when we spoke of planting and harvesting? Yielding to God in your season can bear fruit in you. I thought the Hebrew definition of give up was such a profound definition, don't you? When I dived into the context of the words, I looked to heaven and asked God, "Do you mean to tell me, in my surrender of searching, by giving up and handing over the power to you, I can yield a fruit in my spirit? I can receive a spiritual harvest in handing over the control?" And he reminded me of a time when he told me to quit being stubborn and surrender, which led to the growth and change I was searching for. Amazing, isn't it?

This led me to wonder, why is giving up so hard? I have found that stubbornness is the result of fear and pride. Being afraid to be vulnerable causes one to remain stuck in our ways, which does not allow for change. So when we seek for things, we truly must be seeking for the will of God, which will require giving up our own selfish pride and seek God's purpose and plan for the season. Before I get into this, I need to remind you, I am a student of this thing we call life. I do not claim to be perfect. In fact I have done all of the following that I am about to suggest you quit in this season, I have learned they do not help us grow in our relationship with Christ. Here are three things that everyone should attempt to give up in order to prosper:

1. **Pride** - Proverbs 16:18
2. **Prejudices** - 1 Samuel 16:7
3. **Plays for control** - Psalm 95:1-5

PRIDE

There is good pride and there is arrogant pride. Let me be clear, I am speaking of arrogant pride that is painful to be around. The conceited, indulgent sort of pride takes away from God and puts a person front and center. It is an ego issue. It means being vain about accomplishments and troubles. There are many scriptures about pride. The quote about pride going before the fall is found in Proverbs 16:18. God even finds pride and arrogance evil (Proverbs 8:13). And those who quit being prideful, God blesses (James 4:6). So, if you are searching for God, searching for answers, solutions, love, or people, I am going to challenge you to give it up in surrender to God. Allow your pride to take a backseat to God's provision and direction. If strife is following you in your search, take note, this is confirmation that God is not in that search. When you give up searching with pride, you will find peace. It will flood your heart and overwhelm your body. You will no longer feel torn up inside; you will realize that not having that answer is OK because God is in control.

PREJUDICES

Give up on prejudices. Just quit it. We all have prejudices to some extent, and sin is no exception. Some are really bothered by lying, others by adultery. There are many sins mentioned that anger God. None are mentioned to bring shame, guilt, or condemnation to you. I only mention them so that we are aware of our own prejudices and recognize that God views them all as equal, with none being greater than another. So it is with anger, backbiting, bitterness, boasting, brawling, divorce, drunkenness, envy, fornication, greed, judging, lust, murder, mockery, swearing, pride, and wrath. There are many others, but I am not going to list them all. Today I just want you to be aware and ask yourself: What sins really bug me? Which sins do I have a higher tolerance for? Which ones do I not even consider as displeasing to God? Can you surrender that sin over to God? Can you begin to work on giving up that prejudice to God? This is the time and place to ask God to come into your heart and help you identify WHY that sin bothers you so much. Next, how to you begin to give it up in surrender to the Lord? He loves you and has no judgment against you for feeling the way you do. Just be honest with him, confess it to him in your prayer closet, surrender it to him, and accept his grace and mercy in return.

PLAYS FOR CONTROL

If given a choice I will choose to drive rather than not. I prefer to have a semblance of control when I get behind the wheel. Hence, I have a confession to make. I have a tendency to want to control as much as possible in my life through list-making and driving. It gives me a sense of power and control. Now that my confession is out of the way, let's dive into why we should quit seeking for power plays with control. There's only one problem when I do this: I fail to acknowledge that God is sovereign. He is in absolute right and perfect control of the earth and all of creation. His knowledge is perfect and has perfect power over all (Psalm 95:1-5).

When searching for strength, God infuses. When searching for protection, we are clothed in armor.

When searching for direction, He provides a path. When we give up, He takes over and guides to green pastures to rest (Psalm 23).

When we give up our prejudices, He opens our heart to love people as he created them, not as we want them to be. When we quit trying to control our situation, He provides the path that we are to follow.

Let us pray for this season of searching and giving up the search:

Dear God,

I seek your presence today. I am searching for answers only you can provide. Please help me, strengthen me to let go and give up the toxic that I have been holding on to. I am searching for a safe place to lay down my head, the green pastures of my heart. Please show me where it is safe to lay down and give up so that I can rest. Restore me God; revive the joy, peace, and love so that I may live a life of abundance and prosperity. You are the anchor to my soul, the sunlight to every season of my life. Thank you, Father, for being with me as I examine myself. I give up my attitude and seek yours instead. Create in me a clean and pure heart, oh Lord.

In Jesus' name I pray...

Amen

"You have searched me, Lord, and you know me.
You know when I sit and when I rise;
you perceive my thoughts from afar."

Psalm 139:1-2 (NIV)

Exercise _____

What are your observations about this scripture?

How can you apply it to your life?

How does it apply to searching and giving up in your current season?

_____

_____

_____

_____

_____

_____

CHAPTER 11

KEEPING WHAT'S PRECIOUS

"A time to keep and a time to throw away."

Ecclesiastes 3:6b

As a parent, it is my responsibility to keep watch over my children, to ensure their safety, well-being, and health. And then, they get ready to leave the nest: for school, the military, missions, the streets, jobs, or relationships. It is here that I have to cast my fears for my children and their well-being into the hands of God. It is here that we have to throw away the normal parenting routine and recognize that the once-baby is now ready to fly and stumble on their own. As a mom, I pray that they are keeping out of trouble and not throwing away caution. At this point, the season can feel strangely void and empty while I figure out where to keep my energy and focus as I have one less person to schedule for. Even if though there are other children in the home, the time and energy it takes to focus on the one, seems to not realign itself with the others right away. This led me to ask myself, what do we keep in this season and what exactly are we supposed to throw away?

Are you keeping trash or treasure? Are you littering your season with damaged goods? Or are you holding onto the valuable treasure deep within you? Is your space cluttered with thoughts, habits, and people that no longer serve you in this season? Is it time to simplify your life? Marie Kondo says, *"Never discard anything without saying thank you and good-bye."* (Liles, 2020) Now, this may sound silly, but it actually lines up with the word of God which says, *"In everything give thanks"* (1 Thessalonians 5:18).

We are to keep these things in this season:

1. Jesus' commands (John 14:15, 21)
2. Keep watch (Matthew 26:41) for the enemy (1 Peter 5:8)
3. Your confidence in Christ (Hebrews 10:35)

There are at least 49 commands Christ issued for a prosperous life. In no way, shape, or form are these commands to be perfected, but they are targets to aim for in our daily lives. For the purpose of keeping this short, I want to just go over a few crucial ones to help you through this season:

1. **Follow Jesus (Matthew 4:9)**
   You can't really go wrong when you follow Jesus. He is the target we aim for. He knows that we are human and will fall short, as all will fall short of the glory of God. But, we must try. God justifies you through faith in his son (Romans 3:24). Even when you fall, keeping a measure of faith, even as small as a mustard seed, will keep you safe from harm.

2. **Keep your word (Matthew 5:37)**

   "Let your yes be yes. Let your no be no. Anything more than this comes from the devil" (NLV). In other words, keep it simple. Let your walk and talk match up. If you say you will do something, follow through. Even in the uncomfortable, you can grow. In fact, it will draw out of you a new strength, a new faith that requires you to level up as you keep pressing forward in this season.

3. **Forgive those who offend you (Matthew 18:21-22)**

   Talk about eating humble pie. This pie looks disgusting to those who do not know the goodness of the inside. It is moldy, crusty and has this crazy odor that smells like vomit and manure. But the taste? It is like the candy that has the mystery flavors. You think it's going to taste like vomit, but it ends up tasting like the sweetest fruit you've ever eaten. That my friend, is the flavor or forgiveness. The goodness of humble pie is infused in the aftertaste. The less deserving the other person is of it the uglier and smellier the pie, BUT, the sweetest flavors await you.

   The healing properties of the pie, have eternal consequences. It is a fountain that never runs dry. The more you forgive, the less you weigh spiritually, emotionally and physically.

Keep watch for the enemy, for he seeks to devour you. This means you must stay woke in the spiritual realm. The devil is always prowling, seeking to devour you. Keep watch for the ways he seeks to destroy you. It will be familiar and it will be a common thread of lies that has permeated your entire life. The same phrase spoken over you, coming from different people, is a lie from the devil. Keep watching and when you recognize it, use the scripture that says the opposite. Use the word of God, just like Jesus did, to defeat the devil. A quick search online will help you find the right scripture. Declare "It is written:" before each scripture. Memorize the scriptures; these are your weapons for spiritual defense when the enemy attacks. These are Gods promises to you. Keep them close to your heart.

The promises of God, are only hints of hope if you remain confident in who Jesus is. In believing that he will never leave you or forsake you. Even when you threw away his love. Girl, we have all done it. There is no shame or condemnation in admitting it. Paul wrote to the church to encourage them that nothing can separate us from the love of God, even when we put him in the trash. "And I am convinced that nothing can ever separate us from God's love. Neither death nor life, neither angels nor demons, neither our fears for today nor our worries about tomorrow- not even the powers of hell can separate us from God's love. No power in the sky above or in the earth below- indeed, nothing in all creation will ever be able to separate us from the love of God that is revealed in Christ Jesus our Lord".

Keep this confidence tucked deep in your heart for the darkest moments, for every season that challenges you to believe in yourself.

THROWING OUT THE TRASH

What to throw away? Have you ever looked at the mess of your room and wondered where to start? Jesus help me. I had to clean my daughter's room and it was so messy and I was so overwhelmed my head hurt and ears rang from the stress of it. Three bags of trash were taken out of her room that day. We sat in amazement and exhaustion at the end of the day. The transformation from messy and dirty to clean and organized helped ground my daughter. As she snuggled into her clean bed that night her demeanor was calm, pleasant. There was no hint of the angry, stressed out ten year old. It made me realize just how important an uncluttered and clean room is important not only for our physical well-being, but our spiritual as well.

The mess in her room caused three things to be evident about the trash in her room. It caused her to worship things other than God. Her stuff became her idol. Because it was so messy she often could not find what she wanted the most, which caused her to feel fear and worry. This fear and worry, led to angry outbursts which led to discord between her and other family members. This meant more distractions of attitude adjustments and seeking the lost items rather than peaceful confidence we had stressful evenings of discord. This is where she learned the hard lesson of idols.

HONORING IDOLS

Anything you place first in your life, these are your idols. When God comes after all the rest of life. God is not first, and thus, all other things are idols. My pastor once said this, *"What is the first thing you think of when you become conscious in the morning? That is your idol."* So the phone, social media, children, job, partner, fear, hobby or addiction would be your idol. I understand, it is so easy to do, and so hard to redirect back to the Lord. But all God says, it come back to me. *"O Israel,"* says the Lord, *"if you wanted to return to me, you could. You could throw away your detestable idols and stray away no more"*. God wants you back. He wants your attention. He loves you. In fact, he has chosen you and will not throw you away (Isaiah 41:9).

HATING FEAR

Fear and worry, these are just the beginning of the trashy thoughts that enter our minds. Would you allow trash to build up in your home? How about your car? Dirty, greasy wrappers covered in crumbs with cockroaches that skitter around and hide in the crevices? No right? Or, are you thinking, "Court, you don't know what it's like"…Yes, yes I do. I have found those same wrappers discarded around my home and car. And you know what? We have to take them out to the trash where they belong. You do not need that cluttering up your space. It makes it stink and attracts pests! No amount of air freshener is going to get rid of the smell if you do not take out the trash. Fear and worry, these are stinky trash of your mind. Paul encourages his friends in 1 Peter 5:7 to cast all our cares, burden, concerns onto God, for he cares for us. Girl, take out the trash, whatever it may be. Throw that at Jesus' feet. He promises to be the rubbish man and take care of it for it. He promises to never return it. There is a no return policy on this trash. He burns it, so it never has the opportunity to resurrect from a landfill. Are you scared to let go, just in case? Are you worried about what will happen if you don't? Sister, I am more worried about what will happen to you if you don't throw it away. What purpose is it serving you to hang onto your trash? Is it comforting to hang onto the familiar fear because fear of the unknown is scarier? Baby girl… take His hand, and throw that crap as hard as you can. It is in God, whose word you praise, in God whom you trust and be not afraid. After all, what can mere man do to you? (Psalm 56:4)

CUTTING THE CORD

Merriam-Webster defines discord as a lack of agreement or harmony. Now, I'm not saying lay down and be a door mat, but are you hanging on to people who like to quarrel or thrive on conflict? Are you constantly walking on pins and needles around them? It is time to get rid of the close ties to those types of relationships. They are distractions from your calling. They cause you to trip and fall as you are trying to rise. You need strong people in the arena with you.

People who will pick up the weapon and fight with you. Otherwise, they are just a bystander, watching from the arena seat, cheering for you, but not willing to fight with you. Or, maybe they are baiting you, heckling and mocking your every move as you fight your battles. The time has come for you to cast them out. Along with the sarcastic jokes that distract from the message deep within you.

There is one last thing to keep a hold of; the promises of God. *"For all of God's promises have been fulfilled in Christ with a resounding "Yes!" And through Christ, our "Amen" (which means "yes") ascends to God for his glory"* (2 Corinthians 1:20 NLT).

THROWING IT ALL AWAY

It is time. Time to throw away the mindset that difficulty is a road block to success. I want you to think back to a year ago today. What was bothering you on that exact day? Can you remember what you threw away? Or, what you kept? God's promises are eternal. They cannot be thrown away. They are seeds planted deep within your heart that once watered, begin to grow with new fruit for a new season.

You are not powerful enough to throw away your calling from God. You are too precious, and he has kept you your entire life. Now is the time to throw away every lie ever spoken over your life. You are not a statistic. It does not run in your family any longer. It stops with you. You are healed. Delivered. Redeemed. Worthy. Prosperous. You are strong enough to overcome all things. You do not have to keep the generational curses on your life. Toss that lie out sister, it is rank and offensive to your growth!

Dear God,

I thank you for every purpose each piece of trash has served. Please take out the trash of my life. What is in the bag I bring to your feet, I cast away. I ask you to please help me keep ahold of each promise you have made, and every command you have issued. As I watch for the enemy and his lies help me to stay alert to discord and bring harmony to each moment of discord. I ask you to please open my eyes to believe in every promise you have spoken over my life since the time I was formed in my mother's womb. I decree and declare that my life has a purpose, and I vow to keep your love in my heart as I grow in my confidence in you.

In Jesus' name I pray...

Amen

Exercise _____ ✎

What are you willing to keep?

What needs to be kept, but mended or restored?

What are you ready to throw away?

_____

_____

_____

_____

_____

_____

_____

_____

_____

_____

_____

_____

_____

_____

_____

_____

_____

_____

_____

_____

_____

CHAPTER 12

CUTTING THE TIES THAT BIND

"A time to tear and a time to mend"

Ecclesiastes 3:7a

Mending doesn't mean the tear never happened; it shows that something has happened, the tear is now mended and the weak spot is stronger than it ever was before. Susan Cooke Kittredge said this: *"I see mending as a preservation of history and a proclamation of hope."* In life, you may have faced situations that looked torn beyond repair, but God, with his amazing abilities, mended it. That relationship that seems torn and unfixable can be mended when God is the one sewing the garment back together.

At the end of the day, you can either focus on what's tearing you apart or what's holding you together. I don't know if you have ever tried this, but shifting your focus to God in the midst of feeling torn apart brings life back into focus. The tear ripping through your heart stops ripping open and begins healing , the frayed edges ready to be sewn back together. However, mending is a verb, an action word. It requires work on your part as well as God's. You mend a thing because you still have use for it; you end a thing (tear it) because you don't.

TEARING OF THE VEIL

There is one veil that has been torn on your behalf. The veil between heaven and earth; it separated God from man. It was a symbolic representation of our spiritual separation. Because of mankind's sin, we were separated from God. When Jesus died on the cross, the veil was torn, and because of his willing sacrifice, we are no longer separated from God. Jesus bore the pain of our sin, and thus, the veil was no longer necessary. This kind of tearing is miraculous and holy.

TEARING IT UP

You are destined to live with great success. You were created to tear up the world with your own personal message. Get ready. It is time to tear the spiritual ties that drag you down. It is time to violently pull apart the cloth that is binding you. Break away from all that holding you back from growing in your relationship with Christ. In the Hebrew language, one of the definitions of tear translates to "divide by violent measures; to shatter; to rend from factions." Have you aligned yourself with people, places or events that no longer bring you a life of peace, love or hope? If so, it is time to tear yourself away from them.

As I write, I hear the Lord say to you, it is time. If you have been wondering when, when do you tear away from the painful thoughts, people and places? It is now! NOW! is the time. It is time to tear it UP in the spirit realm. It is time to violently take back what the enemy stole from you. It is time to pull back on the access given out of ignorance, guilt and shame.

Maybe you need to go back into a territory that you left and tear it up to take back what is yours. Take your earrings off, girl, put your hair up in that bun and get to it. What space is yours that you let go of because the fight was too hard to fight without spiritual backup? Friend, you are more prepared than you know. You are equipped and protected with the armor of God. You have all of Heaven's armies backing you up, ready to raise hell on the devil and his minions.

> *"'In that day,' declares the Lord Almighty, 'I will break the yoke off their necks and will tear off their bonds; no longer will foreigners enslave them.'"*
>
> Jeremiah 30:8

What has the devil taken from you that you need to violently take back in the spiritual realm? Is it your peace? Your joy? What about your children? Parents, spouses? How about your faith? Were you robbed of your innocence? How about taking back your purity of heart? TAKE. IT. BACK. It is time for an overthrowing of the spiritual powers of darkness that have bonds on your life. It is time to tear them off. Rip them from you, fling them into the fire and be free.

PATCHING UP YOUR HEART

According the Webster's Revised Unabridged Dictionary, mending means to repair, regarding anything that is torn, broken, defaced, decayed, or the like: to restore from partial decay, injury or defacement. Are you torn up, sis? Is your spirit so broken that mending seems impossible? In a letter to the church, Paul speaks of the perfecter of our faith: *"Looking to Jesus, the founder and perfecter of our faith, who for the joy that was set before him endured the cross, despising the shame, and is seated at the right hand of the throne of God"* (Romans 12:2 ESV). In Greek, the definition of mend is to complete, prepare and to perfect. Your shame, the pain, your guilt, that wrenching of your heart that burns in your chest—there is a promise attached to it, one that says it can be mended.

Are you like me? Do you have a pile of heart issues that need to be mended? Girl, let's sit and have a mending party. I need someone to sit with, because I have stuff to mend too. Are you ready to take the time to sit, thread the needle and mend the rips of your life that need attention? This is not an easy task. My eyes are terrible; I need surgical lights to see what I'm doing while I thread this needle. Are you busy? I understand; it is easy to justify our busy lives to avoid the mending process. Throwing away the garment seems like a better solution, right? We can just buy another, can't we? NO! No, we can't. You see, if it were that easy, God would not have told us that there is a season to tear and a season to mend. The scripture would have stopped with throw away or keep. Some of the stuff we kept is damaged and torn, so we mend. There is no one person who is exempt from needing mending. Everyone needs mending at some point in their life and there is no shame or blame in the process.

On the cross at Calvary, Heaven met you and mended you. At His crucifixion, a soldier pierced Jesus's skin. When Jesus hung on the cross for your sins and your very soul, He mended your heart. By His stripes, you were healed.

MENDING THE FENCES

Reach out (Proverbs 17:17)

"A friend loves at all times, and a brother is born for adversity." (ESV)

Being the noble person has remarkable consequences. Even when you feel as though you are throwing away your dignity, you are activating love in the purest form.

Apologize/Ask for forgiveness (Matthew 18:21-22)

"Then Peter came up and said to him, 'Lord, how often will my brother sin against me, and I forgive him? As many as seven times?'" Jesus said to him, "'I do not say to you seven times, but seventy times seven.'" (ESV)

Yes, even though you may not have been the one in the wrong, ask for forgiveness. If you were wrong, your confession may open the door for the other person to feel comfortable in opening up, as well. Your humble spirit will spark interest and grab the other person's attention. If nothing else, you can walk away knowing you attempted to mend the fence even if the other person was not willing.

Talk (Proverbs 16:24)

"Gracious words are like a honeycomb, sweetness to the soul and health to the body." (ESV)

Unspoken words of love and affirmation leave a void in a relationship, while honoring the other person with words of encouragement, reconciliation and peace bring unity to a relationship.

Listen (James 1:19)

"Know this, my beloved brothers: let every person be quick to hear, slow to speak, slow to anger." (ESV)

Some struggle to listen well to others in the heated moment of an argument. Insert the "raising my hand" emoji! However, actively listening to what the other person says crushes division caused by the devil as you try to restore the relationship.

Follow up (Philippians 2:4)

"Let each of you look not only to his own interests, but also to the interests of others." (ESV)

If your conversation was successful and the air was cleared, follow up in a few days with a word of encouragement or sincere hello. Showing genuine affection and concern for others is another way to find delight in the day and hope in the mending.

EXPOSING THE TEAR

There is this thing in the Christian community lingo world called a testimony. Your testimony is an accounting of how God did something particularly wonderful in your life that you find worth sharing. When you mend something, you are attempting to repair or recreate an article of clothing. In this sense, mending refers to repairing something in the spiritual context. Perhaps there is a scar on your heart from a painful relationship or experience. This scar carries a testimony with it. Your testimony tells of how God stepped in, showed up and saved that article. Whether that "article" is your marriage, job, heart, finances, children or soul. The scar bears the proof of mending, is a testimony to how God put the pieces back together. The patch that covers the hole adds character, life and interest to the garment. I challenge you to bravely share those scars and patches when you are ready.

Someone else needs to see the evidence of God's mending on your heart. They need to know that healing takes place. The scar is the strong reminder to continue to remove being busy from your season and address the tears that need mending in your life. In the future, you will not allow the tear to get so big, because now you know. You will begin the work of mending sooner.

Tearing apart from that which is no longer serving you, and then mending the relationships that are critical to your spiritual growth, have miraculous effects that will follow you as you dance from glory to glory. Your incredible transformation from doing the work of tearing and mending will cause you to break free from your season of winter into a season of spring.

Holy Father,

I come to you today because someone tore apart my heart. I ask you to forgive me for my own actions that may have caused someone else's heart to be torn. Please help me be a better person as I move forward today. I ask you to bless those who persecute me. I trust you to mend my heart as I grow in my relationship with you. As you reconstruct my life and my heart, I ask you to restore and renew my accusers as well. I pray for a complete 180 in their life. May they lay down their life and pick up your cross as I continue to do the same for you. Your mercies are new every day and I thank you for each stitch you are performing on my heart. You have restored my soul, placed me on paths of righteousness for your namesake. I bless you, Lord, with all that I am, I thank you for my life.

In Jesus' name I pray...

Amen

Exercise

Jesus tore the veil so you can be saved. How is Christ being reflected in you through this season?

_____

_____

_____

_____

_____

_____

_____

_____

_____

_____

_____

_____

CHAPTER 13

COMMUNICATING EFFECTIVELY

"A time to be silent and a time to speak."

Ecclesiastes 3:7b

"We will remember not the words of our enemies, but the silence of our friends."

Scruggs, 2018

This statement by Martin Luther King Jr. has never been truer than in this time and place in society. The ability to express ourselves has never been easier thanks to today's technology. With the evolution of smart devices, social media platforms and apps, humans have never before been able to communicate on so many different levels. While this is great on many levels, I have wondered if perhaps the need to be heard has cluttered people's messages and the gift of gab has turned into the "wha wha wha" of the teacher from Charlie Brown. Instead of a clear declaration, the message is now a murmur in the background: undefined, misunderstood and jumbled.

Communication is critical to human development. Babies learn how to communicate from their caregivers and give off cues long before they can form a sentence. They watch and wait for the caregiver to pause and if they wait long enough, an infant will try to mimic them. The need to be not only heard but understood affects the self-esteem of so many. When I feel misunderstood, this is often when arguments arise because I feel the need to speak until I feel validated. But sometimes the only person who can validate me, and not my feelings, is Jesus. This is where so many of us, myself included, go astray.

This is why understanding when to speak and when to be silent is so powerful. Sharing God's truth and your testimony are two very important times to speak. Other times being silent is the most powerful option you have. Open mouth, insert foot. This is something I have an affinity for. I struggle with when to stay silent versus when to speak. This often leaves me feeling like a complete idiot and like that awkward chick that nobody wants to talk to. That's me … she's me. However, I am here to tell you when I am not busy shoveling my foot into my mouth, profound messages pour out. These are usually from God. For me, the time to speak is when it's God's word and His message. And the time to shut up is when foolish speech is about to spew out. I have learned that our words have extreme value and even more power than we even realize at times. And we are encouraged by the Apostle Paul to *"let no corrupt talk come out of our mouths, but only such as is good for building up, as fits the occasion, that it may give grace to those who hear"* (Ephesians 4:29 ESV). What you have to say matters; it is your testimony to God's glory and it does need to be shared, at the right time, with the right people. God gave us the power to speak life or death into situations (Proverbs 18:21). He can and will grant you the wisdom necessary to know when to speak and when to stay silent. That wisdom is learned through one simple act: listening.

STOP TALKING AND LISTEN

Silence is a very powerful form of communication. When used properly, it can stop discord, division and destruction. Titus 1:11 says, *"They must be silenced because they are disrupting whole households by teaching things they ought not to teach— and that for the sake of dishonest gain."* Do you know someone who talks their way into trouble? There is always someone who wants to stir the pot by speaking words that cause division, discord and, sadly, destruction into the lives of others and eventually themselves. As Christians, we are warned against doing so many times in the Bible (Matthew 10:20). Keeping silent also allows God to speak on your behalf; He is your defender when you are facing someone who only wants to cause division. Funny enough, causing discord through conversation has been around for centuries. Even Paul wrote a letter to his friend Peter, trying to help him lead a group of people who were being troublesome. *"For it is God's will that by doing good you should silence the ignorant talk of foolish people"* (1 Peter 2:15).

Walt Disney once said, *"The way to get started is to quit talking and start doing."* (Philosiblog, 2012) This same man was fired from The Kansas City Star because his editor felt he *"lacked imagination and had no good ideas."* (Gillett, 2015) Disney understood the importance of the season to speak and to stay silent. In between the two is something called growth. Not everyone needs to know your business, feelings or opinion on the matter. Staying silent allows you to move without shade being cast upon you. Not everyone is a genuine cheerleader. Many will listen just so they can turn their back on you and curse your movement. Stay silent as you move and only share with those who are critical to the project and the season. If that means you don't tell your best friend, partner, siblings or parents, then don't. It may feel unnatural to begin with, but trust me, growth requires maturity and a lot of times, that comes with a detachment from the norm. Use your own discernment and keep going. There will be those who doubt you simply because what you are called to do is so great, they cannot comprehend it. Do it in spite of the doubting Debbies who sling disbelief like its confetti on New Year's Eve.

Remain silent when you are angry (James 1:19). It is a sign of great wisdom (Proverbs 29:11). Refrain from speaking evil (Proverbs 21:23). When you are listening to advice, remain silent so that you too can gain wisdom (Proverbs 19:20-21). Yes, there will be times when you must be silent and let Jesus advocate for you. Remain silent to the ones who wish only to stir the pot. You are strong enough to withstand the storm of gossip. You are capable of changing gears and realigning yourself with people who will be there for you in support and love.

Keep your peace and have complete trust that God will turn the shouts and whispers of judgment into a beautiful story for you. He will tell the truth in the courtrooms of heaven. The accuser you are dealing with must face your advocate (Jesus) and judge (God) and all must pass through Him. There is only one lawgiver and judge, the one who is able to save and destroy (James 4:11-12), but who are you to judge your neighbor? This is why speaking your testimony is so powerful.

SPEAKING UP

1 Corinthians 4:13 says this, *"It is written: 'I believed; therefore, I have spoken.'"* Since we have that same spirit of faith, we also believe and therefore speak. The cool thing, though, is that God's truth NEVER changes. It is the same yesterday, today and tomorrow. It is a rock-solid guarantee that we can trust Him in all that He says and does. There are times when speaking the truth is the best way to speak. Paul himself was

cautious after years of personal experience to only speak about what Christ has done in his life (Romans 15:28) and always in love (Ephesians 4:15).

God's truth: what exactly is it? Jesus equates Himself with "the truth" in John 14:6-7. In this verse Jesus says, *"And I will ask the Father, and he will give you another advocate to help you and be with you forever— the Spirit of truth. The world cannot accept Him, because it neither sees Him nor knows Him. But you know Him, for He lives with you and will be in you."* By accepting Jesus into your hearts, you are asking Him to be true to you. And in this scripture, He is promising you that the truth will be in you. The responsibility that is placed upon you is to be a good example of what that truth looks like as you walk in each season. Do not get it twisted; perfection is not the point here. The point is to aim for the bullseye of speaking God's truth in a timely manner. When you fall short, God's grace is sufficient to help you. You see, even King David knew that he should speak of God's true nature. In Psalm 40:10 he cries out, *"I do not hide your righteousness in my heart; I speak of your faithfulness and your saving help. I do not conceal your love and faithfulness from the great assembly."* David is known for having made some major mistakes and poor choices, yet he knows that it was God's faithfulness that brought him out of those low places and helped him find peace and joy again. This is why he wrote so many psalms that include words of praise.

Speaking words of praise to God is another example of what to speak. When you are staring at the bill that is larger than all the money you make in a month, speak words of praise. When you doubt yourself, speak this, *"I praise you because I am fearfully and wonderfully made; your works are wonderful, I know that full well"* (Psalm 139:14 NIV).

> *"I praise you because I am fearfully and wonderfully made; your works are wonderful, I know that full well."*
>
> Psalm 139:14 NIV

Praise unlocks your heart. It takes the burden off of your shoulders and chest and lays it down. It allows you to drop the baggage you picked up along the week, baggage that drags you down, makes you heavy-hearted and forces you to take responsibility for it when, in reality, God already has the bag in his hand; you just did not let go of it yet. Drop the baggage, sis, and pick up the praise. Let your gratitude begin to unlock from deep inside. Sometimes you have to find the most mundane, boring things to be thankful for. I, too, have done this when I felt like it was a struggle to find something to praise God for.

I have sat, watching my daughter have a full-blown tantrum and been so overwhelmed with stress that all I could do was thank Him or mentally check out. And honestly, my praise and gratitude were probably a little sarcastic. OK, OK, a lot sarcastic with an eye roll or two. But I am telling you, the mood changed. The atmosphere shifted in my home, and you know what, she calmed down. I calmed down too, and we got back to having a good day after a conversation. But God is so good. He says to tell of the glory of His kingdom, and to speak of his might (Psalm 145:11) and when I praised God for my tantrum-throwing daughter, I did just that. Because she, too, is a daughter of the king; she, too, is fearfully and wonderfully made, and God entrusted me to train her up and raise her to honor Him and others. Man, that is a lot of responsibility! Thank God for His grace.

I hate asking for help; it is so hard for me to do. I have learned over time that this is difficult for me because I was taught to not ask for help. And the error in that way of thinking is that, at times, I did not ask God for help. I tried to do it all on my own, and ended up in a deeper mess. There are indeed times to speak up and seek advice, counsel, physical help to get things done. There are other times we need to also sit back and remain silent in the world but not in prayer. Isaiah 41:13 says, *"For I, the LORD your God, hold your right hand; it is I who say to you, 'Fear not, I am the one who helps you.'"* He will help you when you stay silent and when you want to vindicate and explain yourself. His truth was spoken; he has promised to do so.

Your cry for help has been heard. 1 Chronicles 7:14 says this: *"If my people, who are called by my name, will humble themselves and pray and seek my face and turn from their wicked ways, then I will hear from heaven, and I will forgive their sin and will heal their land."* He is listening to what you're saying, sis. You are never ignored by God, but his answer to your cry for help may sound and look different than what you expected as a response from God.

> *"I was crying to the LORD with my voice, and he answered me from His holy mountain. Selah."*
>
> Psalm 3:4

The final thing we need to speak up for is those who cannot speak for themselves (Proverbs 31:8). We are to be their advocates, whether in person or in prayer. We are to intercede of behalf of many. You are called to speak for a specific purpose, for a specific cause. You have a distinct assignment with your name on it. You are called to speak to that generation for a purpose larger than yourself, and you will know it because it will always point back to God and give him the glory.

> *"Speak for those who cannot speak for themselves; ensure justice for those being crushed."*
>
> Proverbs 31:8

One of my dearest friends was kidnapped, beaten, raped and left on the floor to care for herself. She was battered and suffered extreme physical and mental injuries that lasted for years. This same friend will pull her car up to a stop light, witness domestic violence in the car next to her, jump out and intercede for the woman being victimized. She has helped countless of battered women simply because she has accepted that she is called to do so. This woman does what I could never do: speak up and step into the atrocity of abuse. She amazes me with her bold faith of advocating for battered women. My way of advocating is much less confrontational but no less effective. Please note, I am not advocating putting yourself in danger to help someone else. I have cautioned her many times, but she has always been kept safe. This is for God's glory, not hers or my own.

The time to remain silent will not last forever. As hard as it may seem, for as long as it feels, the season will pass. The season to speak again will return. In this season, speak up for those who cannot speak for themselves and remember that Jesus does this for you as well. Your interceding prayers are not a one-way line of communication. Someone else is doing the same for you. Speak up and ask for prayer from those you can trust to do so in confidence. You have no need to explain yourself, just ask for prayer and let the Holy Spirit speak to them in their prayer closet. I will do the same for you. As you read this, know that I am praying for you too.

Now, let us pray together.

Dear God,

Thank you for your son, my advocate, who defends me when I must remain silent. It is so hard to remain silent when others are judging me and criticizing every move I make. Please help me to remain graceful in the seasons of silence and speech. I praise you for every person praying over me. Bless them, Lord. I thank you for allowing them to advocate for me without my knowledge. I ask you to please give me the words to speak when it is my time to speak. Lend me your words of comfort, healing, wisdom and power so that I may be a strong vessel of your honor.

In Jesus' name I pray...

Amen

Exercise

What do you hear God asking you to stand up and speak about?

What do you see God asking you to sit down and listen to?

_____

_____

_____

_____

_____

_____

_____

_____

_____

_____

_____

_____

_____

_____

_____

_____

_____

_____

_____

_____

CHAPTER 14

LOVING WHILE YOU HATE

"A time to be love and a time to hate."

Ecclesiastes 3:8a

There seems to be a clear line between love and hate in society today. What it looks, sounds and feels like has never been more confusing. With so many conflicting messages of what love is, how is one to truly know when is the time to love and hate? Who do you love; who do you hate? What are you called to love and what are you called to hate? Are you truly to be vulnerable or are you to build up resistance to it and hate? What if there really is a specific time to love and hate? How do you go about doing this as a person, family and community? Martin Luther King Jr. was a man of great courage who advocated loudly for the love of man, while fighting for the rights and justice for all.

> *"Darkness cannot drive out darkness; only light can do that. Hate cannot drive out hate; only love can do that."*
>
> Martin Luther King Jr. (2018)

HATING EVIL

In 2018, there were 7,120 hate crimes reported to the FBI. (Hassan, 2019) That means there were roughly 19.5 hate crimes reported across the nation every single day that year. What a staggering number of hate crimes. Sadly, these are only reported hate crimes; there are undoubtedly many more unreported, undocumented experiences of hate. Why do we keep track of these crimes? Because they are dangerous. Hate, and the negativity associated with it, is tangible and contagious. Romans 12:9 says, *"Love must be sincere. Hate what is evil; cling to what is good."* Hate when used as a verb is something you do. It is an action, described as an intense or passionate dislike for someone. As a noun it is defined as an intense hostility and aversion usually deriving from fear, anger or sense of injury. Proverbs 8:13 says, *"To fear the Lord is to hate evil; I hate pride and arrogance, evil behavior and perverse speech."* Let this be the ruler with which you measure evil.

Hate distracts. It causes division among God's people when they hate the wrong things. The darkness of the human heart can only be saved by the light of God's love (1 John 2:8-11). Hatred at the wrong time causes division; it stirs up conflict. This is exactly the purpose of the negative entity known as the devil. The purpose of division of God's people is to make it easier to pick them off, one by one, weakened by their solitude. There truly is strength in numbers; this is why the military has ranks of large numbers. It allows them to be strengthened. Weak armies traditionally have fewer numbers. What God joins together, let no man separate. If negativity can divide a household, community and nation, how strong are its people? If there is no unity among a team, they do not play well. At work, when a group has to work together and there is division, decisions are rarely made well and discord reigns within the office.

In unity, there is strength. Even when conflict exists, one must choose to love the other person. Through this love, one can "wake up" to their own negative behavior and realize that when they are loved through their ugliness, transformation occurs. You are a conduit to God's agape love. This agape love alters a peron's understanding of love. If you have ever been on the receiving end of this love, you can testify to just how amazing it is. Having experienced both sides of receiving and sharing agape love, I can share only this: God will truly get the glory when someone realizes what has happened.

"Let those who love the LORD hate evil, for He guards the lives of his faithful ones and delivers them from the hand of the wicked."

Psalm 97:10

Making the choice to love those who hate you is not easy. It is laughably hard and at times seems impossible, am I right? Several years ago I was a receptionist, thrown into a chaotic work environment with little to no training. We used those interoffice text/chat services to cut down on running around the office to ask simple questions, and I used it often to communicate with those who were very busy and would not answer emails … you know that type. Not long after I transferred a call to the wrong person, I received a nasty message via that lovely little interoffice system. It was all about how dumb I was, and it was clearly meant for someone else. Talk about a punch in the gut. Here I am doing my damndest to do a good job, underpaid and overstressed for sure, and this witch is gossiping about me behind my back. Truly the opinions of others are none of my business,and I do not need others to like me. But this hurt … a lot. This person had portrayed herself as a friend and was always kind to me when helping. So, this was a huge betrayal to me. As I sat and stared at the message with tears in my eyes, I immediately chose to forgive her, delete the message and go about my day. No response was necessary as far as I was concerned. I chose to find the truth of the statement, that I had sent the call to the wrong desk, and ignored the rest. I made a mental note that those types of calls go somewhere else. Within a few minutes, a ping alerted me to a new message. In the message was a frantic, gushing apology, to which I replied, *"Thank you for pointing out my mistake. In the future I will do better to ensure the I am forwarding the calls to the correct person."*

The responses that flooded my message system were apologetic and extremely repentant. It was evident that this person felt horrible. She explained she was under a lot of pressure and snapped at being interrupted (Can you relate? I sure can). I sat in silence, realizing this was a pivotal moment in my walk with Christ. I could forgive her and show her what his love looks like, or I could hold a grudge and add more discord to an already very divided office. My injury was real; the betrayal was awful. As this person left work early, she stopped by my desk with her eyes glistening from unshed tears, and she asked me to please call her when I got off work. She again, asked me to please forgive her and gave me a hug. I needed that. I needed to know she felt pain from her choice, and in that moment I knew she, too, was experiencing pain unknown to me.

As we spoke for three hours that evening, I learned so much about this woman. She became a dear friend that day. I know it sounds crazy, but it's true. As we spoke, she gave God all the glory. She thanked me for being an example of God's agape love to the broken. Unbeknownst to me, this friend was going through great trials in her personal life and it was flowing over into her work life, causing extra stress.

Has everyone who ever hurt me been this expressive in their repentance? Nope. Do I still struggle to forgive and love those who hate me? Oh hell yes. But this one time I did it right reminds me to do it again. God's blessing is in it. Jesus, the one who suffered the worst betrayal and pain ever, tells you to love your enemies, do good to those who hate you, bless those who hurt you, pray for those who mistreat you (Luke 6:27-28). To this day, that friend and I still call each other to check in, encourage each other, pray for one another and share of the goodness of God.

LOVING WELL

His love is the only thing that can pierce the darkness of your personal hell. Martin Luther King Jr. once said, *"Love is the only force capable of transforming the enemy into a friend."* The devil uses our unique insecurities to distract and blind people from the Gospel. He uses partial truth, a false form of love to slowly tear you away from the true love of God. Love in the Greek translation means to wish well, take pleasure in, long for, esteem. The term "agapao" means to actively do what the Lord prefers, with Him, by his power and direction (Strong's Greek Concordance). Peter reassures us, *"No one has ever seen God; but if we love one another, God lives in us and his love is made complete in us"* (1 John 4:12).

Love is something everyone is searching for. As a clergy, I sat with many people at the funeral home after they lost someone they loved. Godly love was evident every day, such as when strangers were willing to pay for the services for a homeless person who was seen often in the community. Daily examples of his love were never more evident to me than in that place.

For many, the funeral home speaks of death and depression, but truly, I never saw more life and love than in the faces of those who came to honor those who had gone home first. The only time to wait to show love is when you have gone home to Heaven. As someone who has wondered if I was loved, I ask you to please take my advice and do not hold back in telling those around you they are loved. Even perfect strangers need to be told they are loved. Paul says to do everything in love (1 Corinthians 16:14). And you will do all in love when you consider all that you do is being done for God, the author of that love (Colossians 3:23).

LIFE, DEATH AND US

Love is made manifest in life, in death and in us. First, God made His love evident when He sent His Son to us. When Jesus was born, His word became flesh (John 1:1) and all of His promises come to fruition (2 Corinthians 1:20). He was sent to be with us and later, bear our sins in death. Jesus was the propitiation for our sins. His act of atoning for our sins satisfied the debt owed to God by mankind for our own wrongdoing. The ultimate act of showing love is to lay down your own desire for the blessing of someone else. This is why John 17 is one of my absolute favorite scriptures. In it, Jesus goes away to a quiet place and lovingly prays for you and I. When you have a moment, I task you with reading John 17 in as many versions as you can. You truly see the heart of Jesus as he speaks to his father about what he must do.

When you lay down your own interests and act on behalf of other people, you are the example of Christ in the world. This is such an honor. You are called to a life to serve others. True leaders do not serve themselves; they seek to serve those in their family, work, community and church. The expression of your love shows others they are significant and important. Just as Jesus literally laid down his life for you, you have the opportunity to do so, figuratively, as well. And as you do so, you will be walking out your season of love. You will soon be touching lives in ways you may never fully understand or be acknowledged for. Here's the thing: God see's what you're doing, and he knows how you are loving someone. He knows how hard this is to do. And he is recording all you do in his book of life.

Dear God,

Thank you for your love. Thank you for sending your son as a sign of your love for me. Your holy plan is always better than my best-laid-out plans. Please show me the evil in my life you want me to hate. Show me how to love like you. Strengthen me to withdraw from evil and embrace your love so freely given. Your grace is sufficient for me. I know that all I do is done in front of you and recorded in the book of life. I am afraid, God, for the evil I have performed. Please forgive me for those things. I trust you to protect me when I stumble and trip in this season of loving and hating. I receive your Holy Spirit and gift of discernment. Open my eyes to the true evil and love in my life. Remove any confusion and grant me your peace in my decision making. May my decisions be pleasing unto you, Lord.

In Jesus' name I pray...

Amen

Exercise

Read John 17

Write your reflection of this chapter. What verse stood out to you the most? What does it mean to you?

_____

_____

_____

_____

_____

_____

_____

_____

_____

_____

_____

_____

_____

_____

_____

_____

_____

_____

_____

_____

_____

CHAPTER 15

FIGHTING FOR PEACE

"A time for war and a time for peace."

Ecclesiastes 3:8b

The greatest crusade is the battle between good and evil. And there is no greater fight than the war for your soul. Heaven and hell battle minute by minute for souls for their kingdom. Heaven's armies desire your freedom. Hell's armies desire your bondage. One brings everlasting peace and eternal life while the other brings endless death and pain. The pendulum is always swinging. Whether the season is now or later, there is a momentum that propels the pendulum from one course of action to the next. A time for war, and a time for peace. What is done with the momentum gained after each season? During war there is strife, bloodshed, sweat and tears. Among this there are glimmers of hope in humanity.

No matter the war, throughout the history of man, there are countless stories of bravery, love, compassion and heroism that would otherwise never have occurred. Each instance of selfless service has shined a light in a dark time. Hope has shined just enough to get someone to freedom despite the raging evil that was running rampant across the lands. Even during times of relative peace, there are inner struggles with which we battle. The mind is the greatest battlefield humankind faces. The mind is where peace and war begin.

The company you keep may appear completely at peace, but inwardly, many of us are at war with ourselves in some capacity. It may be to overcome some form of condemnation, self-hatred, guilt, shame, pain or trauma. It may be addictions of any kind, heartbreak, a recent fight, stress — whatever. We have all had those moments when, as we sat and listened to someone tell us about their day, our minds have wandered to the battle in your heads. Or is that just me? Too often I have taken peace for granted. I was used to the chaos of "busy," and peace felt foreign and uncomfortable. Sadly, peace can be easily stolen if your mental boundaries are built on weak foundations.

Wars are won by strategic movements to take control and possession of valuable land and assets. In this day and age, the war does not have rage on a different continent or county. Nope, modern-day warfare is different. It is in your mind and heart. You see, you are a valuable asset to the kingdom of God. This is why the battle you have fought has been so hard. The weapons of warfare are easily at hand; God did not expect you to fight empty-handed. Remember David and Goliath? David was equipped with everything he needed to fight his own war. Just like David, you are equipped with your own unique set of skills, experiences, strengths and, most important, the word of God, to fight your battle.

> *"The Lord will fight for you, and you have only to be silent."*
>
> Exodus 14:14 ESV

REMAINING SILENT

So, why the war? What purpose does war serve in your life? As silly as it sounds, you war for peace. There are many reasons to go to war. There are economic, territorial, religious, revenge, civil, defensive and revolutionary reasons to go to war. God has heavenly armies that battle every day for these reasons in the spirit realm.

These wars are to defeat an evil enemy that has a single desired outcome: to steal, kill and destroy God's people. Each demon assigned to you knows your weaknesses. He knows each soft spot and exploits it to steal your destiny, kill your dreams and destroy your hope of salvation. The weapons hell uses are lies, shame, guilt, distractions and condemnation. These weapons are designed to slow your spiritual advancement. When you take spiritual ground and praise God, hell's armies retreat because no weapon formed against you can prosper. Victory is already yours. Truth, God's truth, defeats the lies of the enemy every single time. This is your weapon. The thoughts of condemnation and shame that echo in your mind is designed to slow you down. That nasty DM in your inbox, that twisted partial truth of character assassination, is a lie. The text you received with bad news is designed to make you fearful. Declare God's truth of who you are today and win the war on your identity in Christ. Once you believe this, the battle for your character is won. No one can take away your identity in Christ.

There are two ways to approach spiritual warfare: The first is to remain silent and allow the Lord to fight for you. This will sound insane and asinine to some, I know. I know you're thinking, "Really, Court? Silent? You have no idea what they did to me, what they did to my family, friends, etc." Honestly, I get it. I have wanted to defend, justify and speak up too. But there are times we have to discern when to be silent and let the Lord fight for us. It builds our faith and trust in Him. Some battles are so big, we are too weak and small to fight them. This is when you see how amazing God is, how powerful He is. Fight using the word of God in these moments of battle. This is where God reveals himself to you in a new, emboldened way. These battles are for you first, and for you to share with others later; to recruit believers and build up His army. You will help them find hope too. There are times we must battle, yes, and yet there are times when the battle is the Lord's. I pray for discernment right now for your situation to discern which stance you are to take today.

ENGAGING IN BATTLE

The second way to approach spiritual warfare is to engage in the battle. The war that rages internally is a distraction to keep you from reaching your highest calling in life. It is a spiritual battle designed to distract and deceive you into a false sense of security so that you fight in vain, often because you fight with ineffective weapons. *"For although we live in the natural realm, we don't wage a military campaign employing human weapons, using manipulation to achieve our aims. Instead, our spiritual weapons are energized with divine power to effectively dismantle the defenses behind which people hide. We can demolish every deceptive fantasy that opposes God and break through every arrogant attitude that is raised up in defiance of the true knowledge of God. We capture, like prisoners of war, every thought and insist that it bow in obedience to the Anointed One"* (2 Corinthians 10:3-5 TPT).

What weapons do you have at your disposal as you battle? You have the armor of God (Ephesians 6:10-18), you have angels at your disposal to command to go before you and fight for you. God promises 16 times in the Bible to send angels before you to clear a path and fight for you. Ask God to send those angels before you when you are concerned about entering an atmosphere that is dangerous, filled with strife or hostility. In my line of work, I enter scenes of extreme drug use and domestic violence. Many times, I have prayed for God to send the angels before me when I knew I was entering physically dangerous territory. Every single time I met with someone in an altered state of mind with a history of violence, the meeting went well and the person was cooperative and civil. It would astound my coworkers that I would be in knowingly intense situations that turned out peaceful and easy, while their experiences with the same person were hostile and confrontational. All glory to God that He honors our requests. In the verses mentioned in the Bible, God sends angels to take care of the evil that lays in wait to trip you up. He dispatches his angels for your protection, for your blessing and to minister and heal you. In these moments, you will feel the tangible touch of heaven on your life. It builds your faith, soldier.

You are equipped with everything you need to be successful spiritually, financially, mentally and physically. God's got you.

GOD'S MESSAGE TO YOU

"My daughter, you must pick up your weapons and use them. They are useless sitting on the bench while you watch the battle from far away. In order to win, you must engage. As scary as that sounds, you are ready. You are more than a conqueror and now is your time to shine, sweetheart. You are called to reach, revive and restore through the battlefield into the peaceful meadows beyond. The life-giving waters flowing through the meadow are for you to share. This season of battle is temporary; it too shall pass. Once you are past it, you will look back and say, "Oh!" and see all the little

ways that I was beside you. Trust me, my daughter, I am beside you now. I speak life, love and blessing over you as you sleep. I keep watch as you go about your day. I protect you even when it feels like I am punishing you. I promise you, love is secured. You are my precious daughter, beloved and treasured. I, the Lord, YOUR God, love you deeply."

> **"Fear not, for I am with you; be not dismayed, for I am your God; I will strengthen you, I will help you, I will uphold you with my righteous right hand."**
>
> Isaiah 41:10 ESV

There was a season in which I was battling in every area of my life. Spiritually, mentally, physically, I was under attack at home, church, work and relationships. It was so overwhelming that I began to be extremely anxious and depressed. It was during that season when I had a vision of a battlefield. In this battlefield, I was standing among a battle with war raging around me. As I stood, I looked down and saw a long lizard wrapping itself around my feet, like a boa constrictor. It was green and had the most evil eyes I had ever seen. At the same time, flaming arrows were raining down around me; however, none came close to me. As the vision ended, the Lord reminded me of this scripture in 2 Chronicles 20:17: *"You will not need to fight in this battle. Stand firm, hold your position, and see the salvation of the Lord on your behalf, o Judah and*

Jerusalem. Do not be afraid and do not be dismayed. Tomorrow, go out against them, and the Lord will be with you" (ESV). You see, I was terrified in that vision, as the strange lizard wrapped around my ankles, I had a knowing that I was standing on the battlefield; waging war against an enemy who was relentlessly trying to stop me.

This is when I realized I needed to get armored up and battle strategically, or else I was going to be eaten alive by the evil trying to trip and constrict me. I had to learn how to believe that I was a conqueror through Christ. Paul tells us in Romans 8:37 that we are MORE than conquerers through him who loved us. When we are battling with Jesus by our side in our hearts, in prayer, worship and praise, we are conquering. When we are blessing our enemies through gritted teeth in obedience to Christ, we are already winning. Imagine when you pray for your enemies, you are pouring holy water on the demons trying to drag you down.

Jesus has a teaching moment with his disciples in which he tells them how blessed a person is for believing in Him. At the time, He was healing the multitudes, regardless of who they were or what their past was. In Luke 6:18 it is said that, *"Even those who were disturbed and troubled with unclean spirits, and they were being healed [also]"* (AMP). Jesus did not discriminate in his healing, and neither should we discriminate when we pray. To truly win the war, we have to take on those with unclean and troubled spirits who hurt us, and bless them. This is how we truly win the war, friends. Jesus continues by saying, *"Invoke blessing upon and pray for the happiness of those who curse you, implore God's blessing (favor) upon those who abuse you [who revile, reproach, disparage, and high-handedly misuse you]"* (Luke 6:38 AMP). If you want to win the war for your healing and peace, this is a great place to start.

I want you to take a minute and think about this. Jesus taught his disciples a lesson about the healing power of believing in Him. He was then arrested for political gain and brutally tortured. He was an innocent man who had broken no law, but had healed thousands. He was then left to die a criminal's death on a cross, a willing sacrifice for the sins of not just a few, but the world from that moment on until today. The night before He was arrested, Jesus spent time in prayer, praying for you, specifically, as one who believes His message. He knew His fate would bring peace, but it came at a cost that no one else could pay. He paid it with his blood. He fought the battle for you to have peace.

"He has redeemed my soul in peace from the battle that was against me, for there were many against me"

Psalm 55:18

HUMBLING PEACE

The price of peace is bloodshed. Battles must be fought to keep the evil at bay. Since Jesus shed his blood for us, the price has already been paid. The spiritual battle has been won. Now the season of peace is upon you. These seasons will ebb and flow throughout your life. They are to give you access to new levels of faith and spiritual fruit. They are to strengthen you so you may encourage others later. Each battle you fought was not in vain. You are going to help others fight similar battles. Your expertise and experience are what will embolden other believers. Your testimony of triumph will empower brothers and sisters to walk out their seasons fully equipped. Ensure that when you share your testimony, you do it without conceit, but in humility, counting others more significant than yourself (Philippians 2:3). In doing so, you will prevent yourself from tripping over your pride.

Pride can cause many to stumble in their walk with the Lord. It is the largest tripping hazard a Christian can face. At one point in my life, I had some pride that I needed to be delivered from. Stubborn and not as humble as I thought, God allowed me to experience how low pride can bring a person (Proverbs 29:23). It was after I was humbled that the smoke from the war was clearing and I could clearly see the damage of the battle. I could also see how it could have been far worse. The Lord showed me all the little ways he was beside me in the battle, which I could not see in the moment. The matrix like reflection of the battle showed me where he stepped in and blocked the arrows as I was facing the other way battling with an opponent. Now, standing in the peaceful meadow it seems so far away and so long ago.

I had to learn how to live in harmony with others, how not to be vain or wise in my own eyes. When you live a life of battle and the exhilaration and adrenaline has slowed, peace can be foreign and uncomfortable. Battle-weary soldiers who come back from foreign soil have a hard time adjusting to peaceful life because it is strange to them. For them, a life in overdrive, in order to survive, is normal. To learn how to live without chaos and movement by remaining still is a hard place to be for them. Peace can feel like a punishment with seeming nothing to do. However, it is in the place of peace that renewing of our faith begins on a calmer, quieter level.

This new level of faith and honor, this place of peace brings a new awareness of God's majesty. His grace and mercy have new meaning. A person here in the place of quiet must learn to listen for His still, small voice. His presence here in this place; where you obtain new wisdom and discernment. In this experience of supernatural peace, you realize it is extra special because it was fought and paid for with the highest price. Jesus tells us he is leaving us with his peace in John 14:27 AMP, he says, *"Peace I leave with you; My (own) peace I now give and bequeath to you. Not as the world gives do I give to you. Do not let your hearts be troubled, neither let them be afraid."* In other words, stop allowing yourselves to be agitated and disturbed; and do not permit yourselves to be fearful and intimidated and cowardly and unsettled.

LEVELING UP

Each time you enter a season of war or peace, you are approaching a new level of faith. These faith experiences are what build you up. They establish your relationship with Jesus. They break you to a new level of humility and trust. I have never felt weaker and more broken than when I was in battle. I knew that there was no way in hell I could fight this battle on my own. I could only fight and win when I relied of God and His army of angels. The Lord of Heaven's Armies is mentioned in the New Living Translation 272 times. You are never alone in your battle; you have the Lord of Heaven's Armies by your side. You are fully equipped to stand and fight with all that you need to succeed. And when you are done, and you look back realizing you fought with faith deep down in your soul, the peace that surpasses all understanding will wash over you, making all things new. Your new level of faith will bring you to your knees in worship, wonder and glory. Welcome to this new level of faith. You are now walking from glory to glory.

Hallelujah! Let's pray!

Dear God,

I come to you today with thanksgiving in my heart. I thank you for equipping me for seasons of battle and peace. As I face today's battle, I ask you to command your angels to go before me into every territory and fight every demonic influence that lies in wait for me. I ask you to cleanse my home from every corner; that the the north, south, east and west are protected by your angels. Holy Spirit, come and invade this place, clear out the debris from the battle. Burn away the residue left behind and wash it clean. Anoint the doorposts of my home, work and places of leisure with the blood of Jesus. I de-root every bond the enemy has on my life. I rebuke Satan and his demons and declare that I am covered by the blood of Jesus. May every soul tie that is bound to me that is not of God be broken in the name of Jesus. May these soul ties be burned by the fire of God, and may there be no residue left behind. I decree and declare my relationships are restored by the blood of Jesus. Mercy and grace are my portion. I am victorious. Peace is my portion.

In Jesus' precious name I pray...

Amen

Exercise

What has God given you to equip you for warfare?

Create a prayer list for those who have hurt you. Pray for them when they enter into your thoughts.

_____

_____

_____

_____

_____

_____

_____

_____

_____

A FINAL NOTE

"Perhaps this is the moment for which you have been created."

Esther 4:14

My dear friend, I hope you have received something you needed from these ramblings of mine. I have pictured God throughout his journey, on his throne in all of his holiness, watching me as I have less than gracefully battled to write this book. I am sure he was amused by my many tantrums and pity parties over the past year. As he disciplined me, I experienced new levels of humility and grace. I truly believe God has a sense of humor. Andrew Murray once said, *"Humility is simply the disposition which prepares the soul for living on trust."* Greatness in God's eyes is humble service, not flashy shows of great deeds. And this book is just that. I was humbled over and over as I wrote this book. I hope my battles, stones and moments of peace have encouraged you to do the same. I pray your levels of faith are filled with angelic encounters and quiet moments with Jesus. I pray for your peace, provision, protection, wisdom, faith and healing as you walk out each season of your life.

Your moment of transformation, regardless of the season, is exactly the catalyst you needed to step up to this new level of faith. The dark seasons of the past were purposed to bring you forward into your calling. The pain has a purpose. I see you pulled out of the room, door slammed shut, sitting in the dark hallway. I see you stumbling through, tripping on your feet and feeling for the walls to guide you. I see you running your hand over the wall in search of the door, looking for the light. The light, though, isn't under that door, so you keep going.

As you walk, stumbling, recognize that this, too, is progress. I see you as you reach the next door: you see the tiniest sliver of light and that flicker of hope is renewed.

You did it. You have made it. God bless you, my friend. I am so proud of you and the person you are.

With love,

Court

CRISIS HOTLINE

If you feel you are in crisis, please call the National Suicide Prevention Lifeline. It is a free, 24-hour hotline, at 1.800.273.TALK (8255). Your call will be connected to the crisis center nearest to you.

If you are in an emergency, please call 911 or go to your nearest emergency room.

ABOUT THE AUTHOR

After facing seasons of hopelessness herself, it is no surprise Courtney Dumlao, author of How She Hopes, took her experiences and decided to share her wisdom with others to obtain peace. Courtney is earnest in her approach to helping people find hope in the hardest of times. After many starts and stops, Courtney earned a Bachelor's Degree in Leadership and Ministry from Grace Christian University. She has worked hard an entrepreneur for over 13 years, and is passionate about helping others reach their goals. Courtney serves in her local community in a variety of ways, including church ministry and as a human service professional.

Not perfect, but deeply devoted, she is the wife of Kevin and mother of three children, Keola, Carson and Khloe. Known as the baker of the family, she finds joy in gathering with family and friends over a meal.

BIBLIOGRAPHY

(1955, March 1). The Sentinel, pp. Quote, Page 9-Column 2.

Berry, W. (1996). The unsettling of America: Culture and agriculture. San Francisco (Calif.), CA: Sierra Club Books.

Dyer, W. (n.d.). Wayne Dyer Quotes. Retrieved November 01, 2020, from https://www.brainyquote.com/quotes/wayne_dyer_173500

Gillett, R. (2015, October 07). How Walt Disney, Oprah Winfrey, and 19 Other Successful People Rebounded After Getting Fired. Retrieved November 30, 2020, from https://www.inc.com/business-insider/21-successful-people-who-rebounded-after-getting-fired.html

Hansen, H. F. (n.d.). A quote by Hans F. Hansen. Retrieved November 03, 2020, from https://www.goodreads.com/quotes/7186594-people-inspire-you-or-they-drain-you---pick-them

Hassan, A. (2019, November 12). Hate-Crime Violence Hits 16-Year High, F.B.I. Reports. Retrieved November 30, 2020, from https://www.nytimes.com/2019/11/12/us/hate-crimes-fbi-report.html

Investigate.com, Q. (2017, May 14). 60 Greatest Quotes by Jim Rohn That Will Inspire Your Heart and Soul. Retrieved November 01, 2020, from https://www.investivate.com/jim-rohn-inspirational-quotes/

Liles, M. (2020, March 06). 100 Inspiring Marie Kondo Quotes About Organizing, Decluttering & Gratitude. Retrieved November 03, 2020, from https://parade.com/971716/marynliles/marie-kondo-quotes/

Martha Graham Reflects on Her Art and a Life in Dance. (1985, March 31). Retrieved November 01, 2020, from https://archive.nytimes.com/www.nytimes.com/library/arts/033185graham.html

Merriam-Webster. (n.d.). Plant/sow the seeds of. In Merriam-Webster.com dictionary. Retrieved October 17, 2020, from https://www.merriam-webster.com/dictionary/plant%2Fsow%20the%20seeds%20of

Murphy, R., & Gilbert, E. (2011). Eat Pray Love.

Parrish, C. (2016, January 27). 23andMe CEO Anne Wojcicki Sees Big Value–And Challenges–In Making A Difference. Retrieved October 17, 2020, from https://www.fastcompany.com/3055402/23andme-ceo-anne-wojcicki-sees-big-value-and-challenges-in-making-a-difference

Philosiblog. (2012, June 22). The way to get started is to quit talking and begin doing. Retrieved November 30, 2020, from https://philosiblog.com/2012/06/22/the-way-to-get-started-is-to-quit-talking-and-begin-doing/

Quotations. (2018, January). Retrieved November 30, 2020, from https://www.nps.gov/mlkm/learn/quotations.htm

Ringer, J. (2019, April A). Laughter: A fool-proof prescription. Retrieved May 01, 2020, from https://news.llu.edu/research/laughter-fool-proof-prescription

Schneider, J. M., & Zimmerman, S. (2006). Transforming loss: A discovery process. East Lansing, MI: Integra Press.

Scruggs, A. (2018, February 16). Beyond Vietnam: The MLK speech that caused an uproar. Retrieved November 30, 2020, from https://www.usatoday.com/story/news/nation-now/2017/01/13/martin-luther-king-jr-beyond-vietnam-speech/96501636/